S0-DZF-317

Walking in the Supernatural

BY

DEBORAH AUBREY PEYRON

With Contributions by:
Mark Peyron and Ben Merk

\# 122 of first 200

Deborah Aubrey-Peyron

Walking in the Supernatural

BY

DEBORAH AUBREY PEYRON

With Contributions by:
Mark Peyron and Ben Merk

Home Crafted Artistry & Printing
New Albany, Indiana
2011

ISBN-13 9780982762127

Home Crafted Artistry and Printing
1252 Beechwood Avenue
New Albany, IN. 47150
Contact information:
e-mail: HomeCraftedArtistry@yahoo.com
e-mail: debinyeshi@yahoo.com

Special Orders.
Special discounts are available on quantity purchases of 25 or more copies.
Speaking or signing engagements may be arranged upon request.
Please e-mail or write to the above address.

Cover design by Mary Dow Bibb Smith
Photographs are authors family photos.
Scripture on cover quoted from
Jeremiah 29:11 and Matthew 10:27a.

DEDICATION

This work of love is dedicated to all my men:

My husband, Mark, who is my pal and my covering.
My son David, who carries my strength.
My son Ben, who carries my heart.
My son Andy, who carries my soul,
My Jesus, Yeshi, my best friend,
who carries my Salvation.

Grace and peace be unto you all.

And for you, dear readers, this book is dedicated for you.

"Beloved, I wish above all things that thou mayest prosper
and be in health ,
even as thy soul prospereth. "
3 John 2

Love and blessings,

Deb

TABLE OF CONTENTS

PART 3

ACKNOWLEDGEMENTS

I would first like to thank God our Father for all these experiences and His Heavenly direction on how to use them to bring others to a closer walk with Him. Then, I would like to thank Him for bringing into my life all the wonderful people He sent to help me!

To my dear husband Mark, for all your help and support with this project. You took up my slack from chores to finances and everything in between. You sat patiently and listened to every page. And when I asked you to write your own testimony, even being the very private individual you are, you gladly accepted the challenge. I thank you. You are my pal, and I love you.

I want to thank personally all the people who allowed me to tell their stories. It is my privilege and honor to put them down on paper. It is my great pleasure to know you, and love you all. Thank you for putting up with me and all my endless questions. A special shout out to Pastor Ivie Dennis, who has called me a "beautiful woman of God" and a prophet, years before I ever had any understanding of what that really meant. I thank you for your patience, sister.

To our dear friends and church members, Holly and Jeremy Ward, and to Bill Mauck. I thank you for obeying God when He called you into service to help your sister in Christ. Each of you stood so staunch and would not allow me to chicken out on this mission.

To Holly for proof reading for spelling errors, and for believing in me. Dear brother Bill, you were the "last straw". When you called late one September evening and told me I was called to write this, I knew you had heard from God Himself.

To our dear friend Karen Jensen, who took countless hours to edit this book for me. Your talents and friendship are greatly appreciated. You have made me a better writer and a better person.

And to my dear friend of over 20 years, Mary Smith, who is also an author. I thank you for cleaning this all up. You did everything from adding page numbers, to directing the writing of the technical pages, and even designed the front and back covers. You are a God send.

Last, but not least, to our dear sons Ben, Davey and Andy, who thought this was a "cool idea, Momma". They knew I could do it.

I love you, one and all.

Shalom.

INTRODUCTION

Greetings!

Come on in!

I'm so happy to have you join me on this journey! After all, we are all "journeying", so we might as well journey together!

Allow me to introduce myself. I am a Christian child of God, a wife, mother of three boys, sister, daughter, friend, family member and apparently, a first time author.

I always thought the first author in our family would be my little brother, Ron, who writes beautiful poetry, or our oldest son, Benjamin, who writes like Ernest Hemingway. Not the Momma! Not the "queen of good deed doers."

After all, who am I Lord?

The bible tells us God searches to and fro the earth for a willing heart. I am willing, Lord. Me, myself, just like when God appeared before Moses in the burning bush and called him to do His work. Moses asks to bring his brother, Aaron, because Moses stutters so. He didn't feel competent to speak before Pharaoh. God did not look at his ability, He looked at his heart. God chose Moses to go and free His people.

In this day and age, couldn't God's people use a little freedom? Couldn't we all use some miracles? And don't we need to be able to recognize them when they occur?

That's what I have been called to write about. Miracles. How I was called to write these stories in itself is a mighty good yarn.

What? Did you ask to hear that story too?

I thought you would never ask ...

PROLOGUE

A few years back, I was minding my own business, working, and raising a family, (three boys and a husband), when I got this "feeling", "a calling", to write down all the miracles and supernatural experiences I have had in my life. And that I should include stories of other family members and friends. I figure it must be for "posterity" sake. When my children start seeing things happening in their lives, they will have a reference point for it. In my natural mind, this is what I thought I knew. So I started writing. Fine and good.

About seven years ago, in 2003, Pastor Ivie Dennis proceeded to tell me I would be writing a book for the Lord. What do I know? She even gave me a beautiful journal log to get started. (I never used it.)

Life went on and another few years go by...

I suffered a broken back. Which was miraculously healed but the medical bills were not. My business was taken over and I was let go at the beginning of the recession of 2008 (along with millions of others in America).

All along the way these miracles kept occurring. You see, I don't believe in coincidence, I only believe in "God incidence." Our family was two years into a home church community, and I started getting this calling to write again. People who didn't know each other or go to the same church started telling me the same thing over and over...

Pastor Fred, " You will write the miracles we've seen."

Brother Bill, " You are divinely appointed to write."

Friend Karen, " I want you to see your ministry...so bold for your faith..."

Friend Holly, " Your fruit is different than others... be grateful for what you have... your time and talent!"

Friend Kelly, " You won't write just one book, but three."
Cousin Gail, " I am so glad you are writing these stories.
I have been wanting to but I don't have the time."

Remember what I said about a willing heart?
Even my precious husband and boys got excited about it!
The only one who was really surprised by all this was me!

At the beginning of fall, 2010, one of our brothers
in church, Bill, called me. He asked for Mark and I to go
on Youtube to see a Sid Roth episode with a prophet. I
promised him we would watch it that very evening. My
husband, Mark came home from work. After dinner we
settled down back in our bedroom to watch the episode on
the computer.

It was such a good message we looked around
for anything else on the Pastor that was of interest to us.
On one site a teaching was found that we felt was directly
talking to us! It was on how to build a communication
relationship with God.

"Rethink your focus and realize why God made
you. Be an influence by studying and preparing. Listen
to what God is telling you! People will be changed by the
council you give them. God will give you insight and
doors will open for you!"

After it was over, I sat down and made a list of
all the people I knew God has blessed with a calling
and provisions. Now saints, this is a formidable list of
people. Then I wrote out at the bottom of the page,
"where is ours, Lord?" As I wrote these words on
9/15/2010 at 10:10 pm, the phone rang!

It was again our brother Bill from church. He
sounded excited! Revelation was coming forth!

"Debbie!", he exclaimed, "A thought just occurred
to me on the way home from a bible study. Deb, you are
really going to write a book! It will be on miracles. This is
why you write so much! God has prepared you!

You have a medical, Catholic and Protestant background. You can explain supernatural happenings on all levels!" "Okay Bill," I sigh, "We will pray about this tonight."

I got off the phone, and Mark was looking straight at me. Without blinking an eye he said, "Prepare yourself. We are going to see big miracles, and you are going to have to get good at writing them down!"

Three days later we went to a birthday party for our friend, Jeremy. Our pastor and his wife were there and a couple of cousins of mine were there as well. By 10 pm everyone left to go home but us. I told Jeremy and Holly, his wife, all that had happened. When I got to the end of the story, Jeremy asks, "So what do you want for your birthday?" I said, "Paper and lots of it!" He shook his head no. He said, "Holly, go get it." Out from the bedroom came Holly with a satchel. She opened it up and presented me with a laptop. The Lord had told them in the spirit to go get me one because I was going to need it. This was a big confirmation.

Holly was now in on the excitement! She said, "Now all you need is one of those little hand held tape recorders so when God inspires you to write something and you don't have pen and paper, you can get it down!" We didn't get back home until after 1 o' clock that morning. My head was spinning! I thought, "I guess I am writing a book!" We prayed before going to bed for God to show us the way.

The next morning I started my prayers. "Okay Lord, I will write your book, but I don't even know a publishing company!" I heard out of my spirit, "Zondervan." I didn't even know how to spell it! Later that morning, I went to do one of my good deeds, picking up a dear friend, Marie, to take her to New Albany to go shopping. Marie and her husband, Kaelin, are missionaries from the Philippines. God sent them to buy our home and that is how we met. Yes it is a story.

On the way to the farmer's market, I told Marie all that had happened. I told her about the word for a publisher that I received earlier that morning. She said to me, "Yes, I know where Zondervan is. It's in Ohio. I can take you there."

We got back from shopping in the afternoon, and she went home. By that time I was trying to listen to every slight word that came to me because they were coming so fast! I felt the need to call my friend, Karen. Her boys' grandmother was dying, and she was distraught. That must have been why I needed to call her, I reason. I thought I had called to comfort her. After we talked awhile she asked how things were going with me.

I told her the whole story all the way up to five minutes before I had called her. She started hollering, "Debbie! Do you know who Zondervan is?" I respond, "They print bibles?" She sighs, "Deb, they are the biggest dog on the block!"

This is where fear stuck its ugly head in and I lost it! I cried, "Why would God send me to the biggest dog on the block?!" She calmly replied, "Because you are the head and not the tail."

That night Mark balanced our account to see if there was any money to buy a tape recorder with. We had $23.00 in the bank and I had $10.00 cash on me.

The next morning, on Sunday, we headed out to do another good deed. Pastor Ivie had called us from South Carolina to tell us our friend Joan, who lived a few short miles from us, was feeling poorly. She asked us to go minister to her and her family for Ivie. We said, "Of course."

On the way there we stopped to pick up some food to take to her and her husband, Bob. I told the lady behind the counter we only had $10.00, could she please fix us as much food for that as possible. "You see,' I said to her, "We are going to see a wonderful lady who is very ill. We just want to bless her and her family." Right then, my husband walked around the counter with Joyce, Joan's daughter, (the woman we are going to minister to). Joyce worked at the food market. She started packing all this food to take over. I kept telling her, " I only have $10.00! I only have $10.00!" The total came to $9.12. "Please pay your bill, and leave."

We took the Steward's, and ourselves, a wonderful dinner of fried chicken and catfish. We had a great time! So I started telling Joan and Bob what had now become "my story." I got to the end of it, and Joan said to Bob, " Bob, go to our bedroom in my dresser drawer, and pull out my little hand tape recorder please. I don't think it's mine anymore." It had fresh batteries and a tape in it ready to go.

When God calls you to do something or become something, you become it.

The people with $23.00 in their bank account did not have to put out one dime for anything. All they had to do was obey. All *I* had to do was obey.

Now all I had to do was put all those stories I had been compiling for almost 3 ½ years into a book.

This is my testimony. Man can argue religion forever, and probably will. But, he can't argue with your testimony, or with your witness account.

Let's get started shall we? I will be praying for you!

Order My Steps, Oh Lord!

" ... for when I am weak, then am I strong. "

2 Cor 12: 10

"Who redeemeth thy life from destruction: who crowneth thee with loving kindness and tender mercies."

Psalm 103:4

IN MY FATHER'S EYES
My Story

Some people, right out of the box, need God's miracles in a big way.

Take me for example.

I was born in September of 1958, eleven weeks premature. I had taken a breath in the birth canal and got amniotic fluid in both lungs. At 3 pounds and 1 ounce and 13 inches in length, I did not have a lot to fight with.

The nurses and nuns at St. Joseph's Catholic Hospital in Louisville, Kentucky, came into my mother's room on my third day of life and told her I was dying. I had turned blue and they couldn't get me to breathe. They could not save me. She was told to prepare herself.

My mother called my daddy at home, taking care of the other two children, and said, "Earl! You bring me my bible and my rosary! Call father and tell him to say a mass right away for Debbie Anne!" She wasn't giving up on me without a fight! Thank you my little believing Momma!

You see, *"when I am weak, He is strong."*[1]

When I told this story to my home church, my friend Lisa said, "satan tried to kill you before you were born." This thought still sends chills down my spine. Praise God for His mercy.

Before I go any further with some of the times I really needed God's intervention, I don't want you to think my whole life was one disaster after another, there have been many happy memories and everyday living, and miracles!

After all, that is what this book is really about!

---

1. See II Cor. 12:9

I asked God why it was necessary to tell you, dear reader, about some of the dreadful circumstances I have been through. In my heart, I heard this, *"If they do not see how far you have come, how will they know how far I have carried you?"* Enough said. He is God, and I am His witness. I carry on.

Because I was so premature, I had to wear diapers until I was four or five years old. Then I only wore them at night until I was between eight and nine years old.

When I was little we had some neighbors that I played with next door. One of them living there was a fourteen year old boy. Sometimes, he would take me behind the bushes and take off my diaper to do inappropriate things to a little 28 pound girl. I was little, between four and five years old, but I knew something was wrong. I didn't have the words to tell my mother. After each incident, I would go to my room. I would climb up on the bed head board and kiss the feet of Jesus on the crucifix on the wall. I would tell him I am sorry, and I would be so good if He would not let it happen again, and again, and again.

You see, *"when I am weak, He is strong."*

One night, in the middle of the night, the mother and her children packed up and left. I was never allowed to go over there again, no matter who lived there. God was my victor.

When I was older and had an understanding for what happened, I forgave them in my heart. It was because of the example Jesus set on the cross for us. When I read about how Jesus forgave the man who drove the nails in his hands, it became a little easier for me to forgive too.

My sister got married when I was eight years old. I used to spend the night with her sometimes. I would still occasionally have to wear diapers. Accidents.

Her husband would change me. He said he could help me to stop wetting the bed. I was not to tell anyone what he was doing, or I could get in trouble. He was my "boyfriend" and this is what boyfriends do. I was nine years old. It finally stopped when I was 12 years old. I remember hollering at him, "I know what you are doing! You are trying to give me a baby!" Brother, my knees were shaking!

You see, *"when I am weak, He is strong."*

By the time I was out of high school, my sister divorced her husband. I am sure this action saved her life. She has not remarried as of this writing.

Fast forward, when I was 45 years old, I was in church with my husband, Mark and my cousins, Mike and Gail. God spoke to my heart and said, "***You have to forgive him. You have to call him.***" I didn't mind forgiving him because I don't want anyone going to hell because of something they have done to me. But, I did mind having to call him and tell him he's forgiven! I was scared! I did not want to call him. I cried and begged.

God is such a gentle god. He waited on my obedience. Crying, I went outside and called my niece and got his phone number. I left him a message of forgiveness. Why? I forgave all so that I can be forgiven of all. I want to go to Heaven too. You see, *"when I am weak, He is strong."*

Because of these occurrences, I was very shy and didn't make many friends. I liked to read (it's safe there) and stayed close to Momma and Daddy and little brother. I am sure I thought there was safety in numbers. In my own world, there was so much to do, such as drawing, reading, board games, cards, and television.

I was raised Catholic and went to private schools. By high school I had more friends than I ever had in grade school. I even had the same boyfriend all through high

5

school. When Gary went to college, he broke up with me. He said, " It's a big world out there you know!"

That's when I met my first husband. He was much older and seemed pretty stable. We dated almost a year before deciding to get married. There were a few things he neglected to tell me until after we got married.

For example, his chronic drug abuse, his violent temper, and all the baggage that came with it. He knew before he asked me to marry him that I was a staunch Catholic, and I did not believe in divorce. He knew I would be trapped. No escape but death.

It was a turbulent marriage. As a Catholic, I was compelled to have children. God blessed us with three beautiful sons. I kept them as safe as I possibly could. One evening, after prayers and I was putting them to bed, the middle son, David, four years old, said to me, "Mommy, get us out of here! Get me a new daddy!" I knew God was speaking to me right out of that baby's mouth! You see, *"when I am weak, He is strong."*

At 35 years old, after a year and a half battle to get custody of my children and keep our home, I was exhausted. I started in college for medical assisting. Finishing school, going to work, raising my children, then joining a convent and doing missionary work were all my goals. Of course I didn't ask God about these goals. I thought they were so noble God must approve! It seemed, He had a few minor changes to make. No convent. God needed me out in this world to do His mercy work.

There was a very nice man named Mark Peyron who genuinely needed a wife and three little boys! He was raised with four sisters and one little brother whom he dearly loved. He needed to even the odds! We all fell deeply in love with each other and after a couple of years of dating, we married. Now we were again a family of five! Restoration! I had sincerely asked God for my life to be settled before my 41st birthday. Seven weeks under the "due date" we married. Whew!

My husband, Mark, to the boys "Mark Dad", has been an instrumental part of all our healing. Mark was called at 35 to a covenant walk with God. With prayer and determination we have made it through the teenage years, the unexpected death of Mark's father, the death of a 17 day old nephew, my broken back that healed miraculously before his very eyes, two of our sons recovery from drug addiction (three years + clean!) and losing my job at the beginning of the recession.

This brought us up to where God started working on my heart to write about extraordinary experiences that had happened in my life or the lives of those around me.

I am a natural born story teller, I am Irish on one side and native American on the other. Both peoples have wonderful oral traditions of passing down stories one generation to the next. My father, Earl, my brother Ron, myself, and my son Ben seem to revel in telling stories in writing.

I love hearing a "good yarn" as well. I learn best when I write down what I'm hearing. Nursing school taught me to write and learn very fast! Now my lap top does that for me. I take notes at church, family and friend gatherings. It is my second nature to write. God gave us gifts. Our lives work best when we use them and try not to take them for granted. Anything can become a story. Which in turn can be an opportunity to witness for God and His restorative powers through all things.

My immediate family, mother, father (deceased), brothers and sister are a very good family. I also have a wonderful extended family of in-laws, friends, and church family. In my heart, they are all family. Not bad for a little girl who didn't have two friends at 12 years old! When Mark, the boys and I lived on Mathes Road, our home in the country God blessed us with, we used to have Christmas Open House. I would cook for three days and then open up the doors! We would welcome anywhere from 80-110 people throughout the day. The theme was always an "Old Fashioned Christmas", much like the Christmas parties my mother, Fran, used to have. She was so elegant then, and still is now.

When I was little, satan took my ability to make friends and replaced it with fear. Restoration may take years, but God restored what satan took from God's beloved.

At 45 years old, I had to throw an emergency birthday party for our 16 year old son, David. My ex-husband wanted David and his brothers over to his house originally for David's birthday. He used that time to scream and holler at them. He was trying to ruin David's birthday! They ran out of his house and jumped in Ben's car. They called us on their cell phones upset telling us what had just happened! I said, "Get back home right away! We just moved your birthday party to here!"

I went into action! "Honey!", I cried to my husband, "Go get a birthday cake for Davey. Bring food back with you!" I started calling people. "Emergency birthday party! Emergency birthday party!" I cried! By the time the boys got home, almost 40 people showed up with a gift and a side dish. Our friends and family members dropped everything they had going because I asked them to come to an emergency birthday party. Does anyone else beside me see God's restoration in this?

I don't have to be afraid anymore. When I am the only one standing somewhere, I am still not alone, because God is with me. He is with you, too, and He restores you.

Our sons, Ben, David, and Andy are doing well now. We have no more teenagers. They all have good jobs, are going to college, and have girl friends or wives.

The boys call my husband, "Mark Dad." We are all wonderful, close knit friends. This is what happens when you spoil your children with love, attention, and occasional Walt Disney World Vacations! When they get older, they spoil you back!

I guess if there is anything I would like for you to take away from this story of mine, is that God is bigger than anything that happens to you. After all, *"when we are weak, He is strong."* Whether it be sexual abuse or any abuse, a violent rape, miscarriages, an abusive marriage or relationship, God is there, and He is bigger! He is a restorative God! The bible says in Luke 6:27-28 **"But I say unto you which hear, love your enemies, do good to them which hate you. Bless them that curse you, and pray for them which despitefully use you."** Learning to forgive and go above what has happened to you is an integral part of relationship building with God and man. It is for the good of all souls.

God showed me right relationship building, restoring if you will, when my ex-husband was diagnosed with five different neurological disorders. He had no money for the medication the physicians had prescribed. I myself wrote the paperwork for him to the pharmaceutical companies so he could get his medication free of charge. Saving lives one person at a time, just as my example, Jesus, did when He walked the earth. He got involved in the life of one person at a time. I think I am being called to help many more at a time now.

The only big thing we are still waiting for is the restoration of our home in the country, which we gave up to help other people in need of assistance. God has brought us the land right in back of where we used to live with our sons. Now, if we just knew a good carpenter to help us with this project. Oh, I do know one! Jesus!

If we could only get him to come down here and put on his carpenter's apron, we would actually have our home again! Wouldn't that be a miraculous story to tell?

What a wonderful lead in to Miraculous Interventions - Instantaneous Miracles and Healings.

Part One

MIRACULOUS INTERVENTIONS

Instantaneous Miracles and Healings

"Behold, I will bring it health and cure, and I will cure them, and will reveal unto them the abundance of peace and truth."

Jer 33: 6

PROLOGUE

Jesus forgave then he healed. Just as His Father does. See here, in Psalms 103:2-3 "Bless the Lord, O my soul, and forget not all His benefits: Who forgiveth all thine iniquities; who healeth all thy diseases." Mark 5:34 "And he said unto her, *Daughter, thy faith has made thee whole; go in peace, and be whole of thy plague.*"

Peace on the inside of the body can bring peace to the outside of the body.

I understand in the natural course of events of life we all get sick, but don't we sit above the natural? It's not the question of whether we get sick, but whether we have that faith or rapport with God to know He will bring us from the midst of this. For example, when my heart was healed of hate for my first husband, it wasn't six months before I met Mark, my husband now. I had to be healed of my past before I could move on to my future. Healing had to come.

Healing comes in many forms. It can be anything from a broken heart or a broken bone to a broken pocket book. Nothing is too hard for God!

Jesus called for all to be healed, and preach the gospel with signs and wonders. Your healing is the first sign and wonder to testify to. It is your confession.

These are mine.

A SANTA CLAUS CHRISTMAS

Thanksgiving of 1990 found our family on hard times. My first husband, Clarence, had lost his job. He took a job making $16,000.00 a year for a family of five. That was below poverty wages. Our oldest son, Benjamin, age five, was in kindergarten at the local Catholic school in Louisville, Kentucky. We were renting a 635 square foot duplex from my sister.

I went into the school office the first week of December to let them know of our financial situation. I told them I was sorry. I did not know how we could keep Ben in their school after the first of the new year. Crying, I promised them I was not out spending their tuition money on Christmas presents. The ladies were very kind to me. They told me after the new year, I could help out at the church and school to help make our tuition obligations. I thanked them and left the building.

A few days later, I started receiving calls from people in the church asking questions. "What sizes are your children?" "What sizes are you and your husband?" "Do you own a coat?" "What are you doing about a Christmas dinner?" I thought the women at the front office had big mouths. How did anyone find out about our financial situation? And why?

The leader of the youth group finally called and confessed that our family had been adopted by the church youth group ministry, and they wanted to come over and bring our family Christmas. I thanked them very much, saying that it would be nice to get a little help for the season's needs. I was not sure what to expect.

A few days before Christmas, a van showed up in our drive way. I opened the door to warm smiles and several packages in each person's hands. I asked them in

14

motioning for them to put their packages under the tree. Instead, they started putting them along the living room wall. They went back over and over to the van to get more and more packages! I stood there holding Baby Andy in my arms and little two year old David by the hand as these wonderful people wallpapered my living room wall with packages! Ben, age five, and David were squealing with excitement!

A console television box was brought in filled with food and a 25 pound turkey! By the time they finished bringing it all in, it was well over $800.00 worth of gifts and food. To them, this is what a normal Christmas looked like.

When my husband got home later that evening and came in the front door, he thought he was in the wrong house! What happened? "Santa Claus has been here! Santa Claus has been here!" we exclaimed. "And, we know where he goes to church!" I said as I held out boxes to him, "Here are your Christmas presents!"

Now it was our turn to be Santa Claus to the very people who had been so kind to us. We wanted to thank the group at their next meeting in January. Clarence baked pizzas from scratch. No body can make a pizza like Clarence! I made cookies and desserts. We all dressed up in the clothes, coats and shoes they had given us. The boys brought in some of their favorite toys they were given by the group, and they played with the youth group kids. Everyone took lots of pictures! The group leader said that as long as they had been giving to families, we were the first family to ever give back to the youth ministry. With tears in their eyes, they applauded us.

Benjamin, now 26 year of age, still remembers that night so long ago. He pays the kindness they started, forward, by volunteering at soup kitchens, or blessing homeless people with food, cash or his own coat to the St. Vincent De Paul Society . One day he and his brothers would like to be able to go and give back to the little church on Strawberry Lane. Me too, pal, me too.

A WILLING HEART
MIKIE

While in the little house on Strawberry Lane, our two month old baby Andy came down very sick with Bronchialitis and RSV complications. He was quickly admitted to the *PICU at Audubon Hospital for eight days..

Shortly after coming home, the doctor ordered a bronchial nebulizer to administer breathing treatments several times a day for Andy until his lungs were fully healed. At that time, we had two babies in diapers and a five year old. Clarence was still making poverty wages for a family this size. Our car was very old and had no heat. When we would all have to go somewhere we wrapped everyone in blankets.

One week, it just wasn't enough. There was no way to make our money stretch. There was no gas in the car to take the baby to the doctor, no diaper money, and no money for needed medication.

The boys and I had run errands to the grocery on food stamps. When we got home I fixed lunch for Ben, age five and David, 20 months old. I made a cup of tea for myself and sat down to nurse Andy. While sitting, I added up in my head the bare essential money we needed for that day. It came up to $40.00.

I started crying. I told God that I had done all I knew how to do. Could He please find a way to give us $40.00. I had just finished burping the baby when I heard a knock on the door.

It was Clarence's cousin, Mike McCullum (Mikie). He was on his way to work just down the street from us. He said hello and inquired if we were okay or if we needed anything. I started to answer him when he said, "Wait, it doesn't matter. Here is $40.00."

I gasped and asked him, "How did you know we needed $40.00?"

He replied, "My God told me."

Of course He did.

16   * *PICU stands for Pediatric Intensive Care Unit*

HEAL ME

By 1991, Clarence, myself and our three little boys had settled down in a new home in southern Indiana. Ben was in first grade at the local Catholic school. I thought God had dealt with all the need in my life pretty well. Clarence had a good job, we had a nice car, a new home, etc. I had even started to make a few new friends, something I had not done for years. Being married to a bipolar who would not settle in one place for very long, does not allow a person to make lasting social contacts.

One evening after praying with a new friend, I had a very vivid dream: we were at church having mass, when Jesus came down into the building. Everyone went running up to see him and to touch him. I handed the little boys, David and Andy to Clarence, and gave him Ben by the hand. I said, "Go have Jesus bless the boys!" He agreed and started making his way toward the front alter.

I went to the back of the church, and got on my knees and cried. I did not feel worthy to go up and see the Lord. I prayed on my knees in the back of the church, crying, not wanting to bother Jesus, seeing how busy he was with everyone else.

All of a sudden I felt a hand underneath my chin, lifting my head up. There was a great light all around me. I could hardly see past it. As my eyes adjusted, I saw it was Jesus! He had come back to find me! He left the 99 to go find the one little lost sheep. And saints, He was smiling! In all His glory He was looking at me with love and tenderness and a big, beautiful smile! He didn't say anything. He didn't have to.

All the pain and sorrow I had been carrying from years of being hurt and molested left me that instant. I was healed and whole and ready to go!

The reason? Besides that He made me and loves me, He knew what was coming and what I still had to go through. Shortly, my marriage would break up, and I would be a single mom. God knew I was going to have to be stronger than I was then in order to get through it all.

He had a vision for my life, and this wasn't it. I had to prepare to be in His service to help people, many people. I had to be the first one in that line healed!

What healing can He do in your heart today so you can go out and minister the gospel to others in need?

THE LAST STRAW

In the last few months of my first marriage, things got very hard. I knew in my heart our marriage was failing fast. Clarence had come off his medication. He had also stopped going to anger management classes. It was a trying time for the boys and I. All we wanted was to be safe. It seemed, at the time, safety was nowhere to be found.

One afternoon everything came to a head. I was standing against Clarence, praying during one of his tirades. He yelled, "You will not teach the teachings of Jesus Christ in this house anymore!"

I knew my hour had come. I stood as tall and firm as my five foot two inch frame would allow. Evenly, I said, "You will have to kill me to stop me." That was the last straw. I felt as if I had just signed my own death warrant.

I waited for the final out come. In my head I was apologizing to God, I thought I had failed Him. I asked Him to please take care of my children.

Clarence opened his mouth and took one step forward. Then, he stopped, shut his mouth and left the house.

Yes, indeed. That was a miraculous intervention. I lived. Something stopped him. Angels, I think.

EPHESIANS 6:10-18
"THE ARMOR OF GOD"

By the time I was 35, my marriage to Clarence was over. I was separated and working at a bank in Louisville, Kentucky. Being a new hire, I went in to work sick with the flu. It was going around the office. I thought at that time, if you got sick, you just got sick. You had to wait for the doctor's medicine to heal you.

I had a temperature of over 101 degrees and felt awful! I called my doctor, who couldn't see me because he was so busy seeing other patients with the flu! It was then that I called my boys' pediatrician to see if she could see me. Her office was busy with the flu too! Her nurse, Vicki, who was a strong Christian said, "Debbie, let's pray together, you believe in Jesus." She prayed Ephesians 6:10-18, the armor of God, and that the blood of Christ would wash over me and heal me. She knew I would be healed.

By the time she finished praying, my temperature, aches, and pains, all left me. I was instantly healed! This was the first time I was ever made aware of instant healing. "Wow! Does anybody else know about this?" I thanked her so much and hung up ready to go back to work.

I took my cup of tea upstairs back to my desk and back to work. I went back among all those sick people, and I never caught as much as a sniffle.

Amen and amen!

Even illness has to bow to the name of Jesus!

MANNA FROM HEAVEN

In the spring of 1999, I went to school for medical assisting. The government was paying for our apartment for the three boys and myself, for me to go to school and our food stamps. I am still very grateful for all the help from those services. One month I ran short of food a couple of days early. I had a tendency to feed other kids in the housing complex. I must have over extended that month because our food supply did not go as far as usual.

That morning all I had to feed the boys was a can of what I called "who hash," and eight saltines. We were all so sad. For the first time, I had let my children down. I told the boys to go outside and play. I needed to go before the Lord in prayer. While praying, I felt in my spirit that I needed to ask my boyfriend, Mark, for $5.00. At that time, I could buy a package of hamburger, a loaf of bread, six apples, and a jar of peanut butter for that amount. You know, the good old days. The boys could have school breakfast for free.

Mark showed up 45 minutes later, and I wondered what took so long. He gave me $5.00 and said he would watch the boys until I got back. I thanked him very much and started for the store. I stopped by the front office of our complex to ask a question and saw that there were loaves of bread on the table out front. They had free bread! I asked if I could have two loaves, telling them what was going on in my life. They said, "Sure!"

While I was out believing and thanking God for the $5.00 and now the bread, God was working His real miracles, His favor. His five loaves and two fishes.

After I left the office the girls were upset! These people needed food! They called three church ministries who started packing up groceries and cash right away!

In the meantime, Mark was unpacking $70.00 worth of groceries out of his trunk into our apartment. That's what took so long. While he was there, Clarence, my ex-husband called the apartment. Mark answered the phone. He told Clarence we didn't have any food! Clarence told him he would go straight away to the grocery too and be right over! He brought in $40.00 worth of groceries.

I got back from the store thinking how wonderful God was to have given me the $5.00 and two loaves of bread to get us through. I walked through my front door and there was all this food in the kitchen that Mark brought. Clarence showed up 30 minutes later with his help! Then the three churches showed with food, toiletries and enough cash for gas in the car to last a month! There was also a pizza so big we couldn't close the oven door completely to cook it! The boys and I were laughing and crying. I had a big kitchen, and you couldn't get all the food in the cabinets, on the counters and the kitchen table. It spilled out into the dining room!

So the next time you ask God for a little bit of help, open your arms wide!

OUR FIRST CHRISTMAS

The first Christmas Mark and I were married I woke up sick with the flu. I had nausea, fever and chills. I cried because I was going to miss our first Christmas together. I was going to miss morning mass.

Mark got all the children ready and then gave me a glass of Ginger ale and some soda crackers. He turned on the television to find Mass on the Air. He kissed me and left with the boys. I sat up to watch and pray with the priest. When the blessing of communion came, and the priest raised the host up, I felt the Holy Spirit fall over me three times. I was healed immediately.

I heard a voice softly say, *"Sleep one hour and then go about your day."* I fell fast asleep and woke up exactly one hour later. I got up feeling wonderful!

I cleaned up and dressed, and I went to see my husband at his family's. I told him what had occurred. How exciting for our first Christmas together!

When I got to my Momma's that afternoon, she met me at the door saying, "There has been a miracle in the family! I felt it!" I confirmed her feeling and told her what had happened. Although she was glad I was not sick anymore, she had hoped it was for my little brother, Ron, for his marriage to be restored.

That was not to be.

A CHRISTMAS MIRACLE

In the beginning of our third year of marriage, Mark and I had several people, who were not acquainted with each other, come forward to tell us that we were to go look for land, build a home and even who our builder would be. Since we do not believe in coincidence, we started early in the new year of 2002 looking for land. I wrote on a piece of paper "$18,000.00" and "for sale by owner." That is how we would know the land when we saw it. Mark even got the feeling of where we should drive. When we stepped onto the land, the Holy Spirit fell on me from my feet up. That's it. We were home.

We did indeed buy the land for $18,000. Everything went well and were in before Christmas. We had many bible studies and prayer groups in that home.

By the fourth year of our marriage, and two years into our new home, my back broke, it fractured at LL5, S1. We had no health insurance. The muscles along the left sciatic nerve from the gluteus medius to the Achilles tendon froze. It was like a charley horse 24 hours/seven days a week. All the doctors could do was put me down with medication. From the pain, my temperature would go up to 100 degrees and my hair fell out in clumps. My blood pressure was rising week after week.

After seven weeks of incredible pain, I laid on the floor at 3 am during Thanksgiving week, and cried out to the Lord, "I know you are God. You can do anything! Take me up! Get me out of here! Take me home! I don't want to be here anymore! You can do it! I don't want to be a mother or a wife!" My husband was on the floor next to me rebuking every word out of my mouth. Our youngest son, Andy, was hollering in the hallway, "Momma, stop it! You are scaring me!"

24

I heard a voice as if someone was standing next to me, I believe an angel said, "*Hang on! Your Christmas Miracle is coming! Your Christmas Miracle is coming!*" Being in the frame of mind I was in, I cried out again, "Christmas! It's not even Thanksgiving!" With my next breath, I said, "But not my will, but thine be done." My husband rubbed anointed oil on my back and leg and prayed over me for two hours. I was finally able to get back into bed and sleep a little while until my next round of medicine was due.

While this was going on, I played praise music over and over again until I wore out a CD. The doctor scheduled me for an epidural block. It was Christmas time, and my husband Mark was a bench jeweler. He was pressed for time and had no time to stay and help me afterwards. He took me over to the hospital that morning and the nurses prepared me for the procedure. The head nurse in charge of me blew the right vein three times trying to put in an IV for medication distribution.

When they finally got me ready and wheeled me back to the operating room, the anesthesiologist ran the medication for the block down the wrong leg two times! By this time, I had bilateral inflammation and pain on both sides!

Mark brought me home, and my good friend Margaret stayed with me, cooked us a lovely beef stew and she waited for the next round of people who came to help. My cousins came and brought us dinner. I was in terrible pain. I was breaking out in a cold sweat, and started to moan and yell. At that point they decided they had had enough. Gail told me as she was leaving our home, "Deb, you aren't praying hard enough." If I could have caught her I would have bit her. Don't worry, she was forgiven along time ago, at the cross.

25

The next day my dear friend Mary came and stayed the whole weekend with us. She cooked meals and did dishes, made cookies, and brought me wholesome treats. Anything that might cheer me up, she did. We prayed together and cried together. She took wonderful care of me. Mark owes a debt here he can't repay. It took all the stress off of him. The day Mary had to go back home, our friends Lee and Anne called. They wanted to come and see us the next evening. It was soon to be their 25th wedding anniversary, and they wanted Mark to make Anne an opal ring for her present. It would be very nice to see them.

The next morning while praise music was playing, I was laying on the floor trying to wrap a few Christmas gifts for our children. All of a sudden I heard beside me, *"be very sorry for everything you have ever done."*

I took off my glasses, put my head on the floor and cried for half an hour before the Lord. I had a repentant heart. I did not understand that I was being prepared for what was to come.

They came over, and I was laying back in the recliner. I was sweating with pain. Anne conducted her business with Mark quickly then she came over and sat on the couch by her husband and took a good look at me. She said, "Debbie, you look terrible." I replied, "I know Anne, but I keep hearing somebody next to me saying over and over that my Christmas miracle is coming. I believe I am going to have a miracle sometime this season!" She got really excited and grabbed Lee by his arm. She said to him, "Lee, did you hear that? Debbie is going to get a Christmas miracle! We believe in that too!" Then she looked at me and said, "Lee's hands are anointed like the Apostles." I knew right then and there my time for full healing had come. Lee and Anne looked at each other. She said, "You have to ask him in faith."

I asked Lee, "Would you please allow the Holy Spirit to enter you and heal me?" He said, "Why sure!" as if I had asked him to go get me a glass of milk.

Mark and Lee gently laid me on the floor. All I could see were knees. Mark was on his knees at my feet, Anne sitting on the couch beside us, and Lee on his knees at the middle of my back. He said to me, "Debbie, say a prayer in your head. I will know when to start." In my head I said, "Lord, I come before you humbly. Please find nothing in me that would cause you to turn away." He put one hand on my head and the other hand started down my back without touching me. He was inches above me. Immediately I felt heat. It felt hotter and hotter, until he got to the place that was damaged. I was yelling, "Hot! Hot!" Anne was giggling on the couch. She knew what was coming!

Then the damaged disc area began to tingle, to incite as if it were waking up from a sleep. The nerves were firing up! The left lateral muscle LL5/S1 moved back in place. I *felt* the disc heal, wiggle and move back into place. Lastly, the right lateral muscle moved into place as well. At that point, Lee put his hand on my back and it felt like a "surgeon closing from surgery". All the pain ended. Gone.

Lee sat back. In an instant I jumped up all by myself! I could've flew! I yelled, "Yyyyyiiiipppiieee!" Then I started to cry. We all started to cry. Mark cried out, "Praise the Lord!" It was an instantaneous miracle.
I looked up at Lee and asked, "How can this be?" And all of a sudden it felt like 2,000 years ago as he replied, "Woman, your faith has saved you." I asked him again, "What did it feel like when the Holy Spirit entered you and healed me?" He said he felt tremendous joy. He told me that I had no stoppers and that my faith was complete.

Now, I could stand again and sit. We laughed and cried. Like Peter's mother-in-law after she was healed by Jesus, I got up and served people drinks and snacks. It was the least I could do. The fracture was healed and I knew my sins were forgiven. What a glorious day.

I couldn't speak a whole sentence for three days. I was overwhelmed. My muscles were tired due to the stress of what they had been through, and I did physical therapy in my home with a book we found on line as my guide. The next day I could drive and dress myself once again. I could walk by myself.

Three weeks after my healing, I was laying on the family room floor doing my daily physical therapy, and I was cold. There was a draft coming in from the patio doors. From my side view, I saw a man in white pick up my blanket off the couch and bring it over and lay it on top of me. I said, 'Thank you." No one replied because no one was there. I went down the hall. Andy was in his room doing homework, and Mark was in our bedroom working on book work.

I tell you, it was an angel sent to comfort me after all I had been through.

God, being no respecter of persons, if He will do this for me, what will He do for you? Evidently, all we have to do is ask, and receive.

FOR THE SAKE OF TWO SOULS

I tend to think of successful evangelists as seasoned, well rehearsed, or naturally gifted. It seems they are usually grey haired, married, and have glasses from years of studying scripture to bring people to the Lord. I've often wondered how many people converting under a minister's touch makes him or her successful.

Hundreds of thousands? Tens of thousands? Hundreds? What if it was only two they converted and they did it without saying one single word? Even the youngest of us can evangelize.

February of 2003 was a hard month for our family. Our oldest son, Ben, had moved in January to Florida with his birth father. Fearing for Ben's safety, I wasn't very happy about the decision but he was almost 18. It was not up to me anymore.

My sister in-law was six months pregnant with a boy! They were going to name him Dylan. Danielle, his three year old sister, could hardly wait to hold him!

About mid-February Sandy wasn't feeling well. Mark and I thought she had a stomach flu. I called and talked to her. She promised if she wasn't any better after the weekend, she would go to the doctor on Monday. I hung up feeling better.

By the first of the week, she was too ill to go to work and did indeed go to the doctor. She was diagnosed in Pre-eclampsia, and her blood pressure was sky high. They gave her a shot and sent her by ambulance to a Louisville hospital. In a desperate attempt to save mother and child, they delivered Dylan almost three months early. He weighed 3 pounds and was 16 inches long. He was so tiny that when he cried, he made no sound.

Since I had been a six month baby 45 years ago, I

reassured everyone that if they could save me then, the hospital could surely save Dylan now. The next 24 to 48 hours mother and son seemed to stabilize. The family got to see him through PICU* glass. He was so beautiful! Dylan had lots of long dark hair. Everyone was praying for a good outcome. We called our son in Florida updating him and asking for his prayers.

Near the end of Dylan's second day of life, he suffered a complete brain hemorrhage. All but the base of the brain, succumbed. They put him on life support. He was now blind, deaf, full mental retardation, he couldn't even swallow. He was placed on a feeding tube. We prayed for a miracle healing that did not come. The doctors waited ten days for a sign of anything to come back. There was nothing. Plans then started for taking him off life support. It was time to gather the family.

We called Ben to let him know what was happening. He begged me to fly him home quick! He said, "Momma, if I don't get to see him now, I may never get to see him!" I started calling airliners for an emergency flight home. I was crying. The attendants were crying. We got that kid on a flight for 11:20 that morning! I called him saying, "Pack quick! Get to the airport as fast as you can! Your flight leaves in 1 ½ hours!" He threw things into a satchel, grabbed the first friend he could get hold of to drive him to the airport. Off to Kentucky he flew!

I picked him up at the airport mid afternoon. Ben, Andy and I, arrived at the hospital a half hour later. At that time of the day, no one was with baby Dylan but his nurses. They led the three of us into a small room. All the advanced medical instruments were humming and lights blinking. The nurse advised us not to rub the baby but to touch him or hold his leg so as not to bring him discomfort.

Ben walked up quietly and held his little leg.

I'll never forget what he said to him as long as I live. He said, "I am the oldest grandson, and you are the youngest. I am the biggest grandson, and you are the smallest. But from Heaven, you will watch over me." The nurse took a picture of Ben and Andy holding the baby. Then Ben kissed Dylan gently on the top of his head. We got a picture of that too. The family brought in a priest and baptized baby Dylan. Mark had the privilege of being his godfather.

A few days later, all the family was called into the hospital to say good bye. The doctor came in to turn off the machines and let God be God. Everyone got to hold Dylan and have their picture taken with him. Sandy, his Momma, got to feed him and change his diaper one last time. There was no consoling Hunter, his father. His son was dying and he couldn't fix him.

Finally the nurses came in and unhooked all life support from him. Dylan's doctor stayed to monitor him and be with the family until the end. It was time to say good bye.

While we were all there, my husband Mark led us in prayer, reading scriptures the Lord had showed me earlier that morning to give to him. And little Dylan left his mother's arms and went home. We know in our hearts, Grandpa Dan was there to receive him.

Dylan's body was buried on a cold windy March morning. Soon after, his mother, Sandy, was baptized and his cousin, Ben, had a conversion as well.

A short life well lived.

God can use all of us with no respect of age or ability. You see, God doesn't see or count miracles the way we see them.

Where was the miracle here you ask? Why, two souls saved, of course.

In memorial of
Dylan Peyron Royal
Born February 19, 2003
Bourne into Heaven March 8, 2003

LETTING GO

When I have insightful dreams, they are dreams when I am asleep, like everyone else. They can be announcing dreams, prophetic dreams, words of knowledge, healing dreams, etc. Some are straight forward and others need interpretation.

Our youngest son, Andy, dreams too. But mostly, he is a visionary. Everything I do in the spirit, he does better. Better reception, I think. A clearer path. This may have something to do with the fact that He died twice as a baby and came back, just like his mother.

In 2003, when our son was 13, he met his first girlfriend, Sabrina. She was a cousin to a family at the local Christian church where Andy went to youth group on Wednesday nights. Her family moved to Illinois shortly after they met. They wrote back and forth to each other. Andy still saw her family each week at the Wednesday night youth group.

One day her family got a call that there had been a terrible accident. Sabrina had fallen off the back of a moving pick up truck and hit her head. She was in a coma and not expected to live. She passed shortly thereafter.

We allowed Andy to go up to Illinois with her family members to the funeral. This event touched Andy deeper than we knew. For years he held this in his heart. Each Christmas that went by, he still mourned her loss.

The Christmas of 2007 was a busy one. We had sold our home where our children grew up, due to financial difficulty from bills due to my back injury and the business where I worked was going downhill. We went from 3800 square feet to an 800 square feet rental. We either sold our furniture or gave it to our other two boys, or friends.

A few days after Christmas, late in the evening, when we were already in bed, Andy came in and wanted to talk to us. Being the diligent parents that we were, we woke up quickly, put on our glasses and asked what was wrong? How could we help him?

This is the story he told us:

On Christmas day after we left Grammy Fran's, Ben and I went to see George and Patti. I was missing Sabrina really bad and I couldn't get her off my mind. I laid down on their couch and started praying. The sounds from the television and people around me got softer and softer until I couldn't hear them anymore. Then, there was light all around me. It was so bright that my eyes had to adjust to see. I was in an area, where all I could see was white light. I was standing but not sure on what.

Suddenly, I wasn't alone. Sabrina came walking toward me. I was so excited to see her! We danced together! She told me I had to get over her and that there were things I had to do. I've been sent here. I have to move on. We parted, and she walked away from me towards a bright beam of light. I ran towards her, and I saw stairs in the light. I started running up the stairs calling out, take me with you! She turned toward me and said, "No! You cannot go where I go. It's not your time! You have to finish your mission! I will see you again. Time is short." When I started up the stairs, a great pain hit my chest, and I could hardly breathe.

"Then the bright light faded. The familiar sounds of friends and Christmas came back to me. What I need to know is, what she meant about time being short. Am I going to die soon?" Andy sat patiently waiting for an answer.

34

Then it was my turn to tell him a similar story about time being short.

A few months after my divorce from their dad, in the spring of 1996, I experienced my second healing dream.

Tension was still high. There was a court order that we could not talk and he couldn't come near the house or us. I had a lot of internal pain over all that I had experienced with him. I could not let go of the hate I had for my ex-husband, at least not without God's help.

One night, I dreamed I was in a beautiful garden. The colors and smells were so vivid. My daddy, Earl, who had died when I was 21, was there sitting on a rock in a clearing. I ran to him and hugged him. I cried, "Oh, daddy, I'm so happy to see you! Have you a word from God for me?" He replied, "You have to forgive Clarence for time is short." I fell to his knees crying, "Oh, daddy, I don't want to. But for you and only you, I will." Immediately, I woke up.

I awoke with peace beyond understanding. The first thing I did was to call Clarence, going against the standing court order. He answered the phone, and I said excitedly, "Clarence, Clarence, I've heard from Daddy!" He was not unaccustomed to hearing such comments from me. He replied, "What did Earl have to say?" I told him about the dream and what Dad had told me. "So I have something to tell you. I forgive you and I love you," I stopped and waited for a reply. At first there was no sound. Then I heard him softly crying and sniffling. He gently hung up the phone. Healing had begun on both sides of the fence. With God's help, I let go.

"Now son, that dream was almost 12 years ago. I don't think the Heavens count time the way we count time. I asked God to allow me to live to your 18th

birthday so Clarence couldn't get his hands on you. I do not think it means you nor I will die soon. Please don't worry."

"Thanks, Momma".

A year came and went, Andy turned 18 and moved out with some friends just down the road from us.

On February 18, 2008 at 1:30 am Andy woke us up with a call. He had been to church that night where he had first met Sabrina. He was praying with a friend. Again, Sabrina came to Andy in that church and told him it was time to let go. He prayed, he said good by and then it was time for him to let go.

He felt a release of all he had been carrying all those years. The weight on his shoulder's lifted. His burden was now made light, just as scripture promises.

We cried and told him we love him so very much and how special he is.

Letting go only hurts until you let go.

COME OUT OF HER MY PEOPLE!
Part One

At the end of 2007, the business I worked for was bought. The new people who took over needed me to train people for patient assistance. I trained people and then worked from home. I knew under the new group, I didn't belong there. Even though they stopped my pay until they could refinance, I was expected to help. After ten weeks without pay I could not carry on anymore.

These events coincided with the beginning of Lent, 40 days before Easter. My husband went to a Men's Lenten Breakfast. The speaker was Pastor Fred Schuppert. He had a wonderful testimony and gave out CD's called "Radical Fanatical Christianity." Mark brought one home and showed it to me. I said, "What's this?" By the title I was very unsure of listening to the CD. But God sat on me about listening to this man's testimony. Finally, I sat down one afternoon and listened.

It was so moving and powerful! It was his testimony on all the miracles he's seen just by believing God and the Bible. I truly felt after listening to this man's CD several times over, that I should go talk to him. He would have the answers I was seeking. I had no idea where they lived. I Googled them and found out they lived a few short miles from us!

I gathered up my directions with their CD in hand and off I went on a Tuesday afternoon. I pulled up to a very nice brick home that used to be a photography studio. It was converted to a private home and church.

Jeanne, Fred's wife, answered the door. "May I help you," she asked politely. "I am sorry to bother you, but are you these people?" I asked holding up their CD. "Yes we are" she replied. I told her I felt God had sent me there for direction in my life, and that they could help me find answers. She asked me to come in.

I said, "Wait, I am not a member of your congregation." She said, "We don't have a congregation."

I replied, "I am a Catholic. I am a Charismatic Catholic. Do you know what that is?" It was my understanding at the time that some Protestant faiths do not allow Catholics in their homes. I also didn't figure she knew what a charismatic Catholic was and I would have to do some explaining. When she gave her answer I knew I was at the right place.

She said to me, "We've been expecting you. The Holy Spirit told my husband when we moved here, he would be sending us charismatic Catholics to help us."

I went in her home in tears. I told her the whole story. I got 3/4 of the way through, and she called her husband at work. He came over right away! I was saying the last two sentences of the story when Fred came walking through the back door. He did not need to hear a thing I had said. He looked right through me and saw it all.   That's when he started speaking the word of God to me and I started writing it down as fast as I could! He started, "You are a Christian! A child of God! Why would you want to work for someone who is trying to steal your peace?"

At that moment, I knew I had to leave my job. I quit two days later. I packed up everything and took it all to the office. But back to what Pastor Fred was saying. "This world is trying to destroy your peace. Stop carrying all the weight of others around. It is weighing you down." Wisdom from on high.

I told him I'd be happy scrubbing floors right now. Boldly he declared, "You were not made to scrub floors!" Then he really started prophesying, and my tears started flowing.

Fred looked like the lion of Judah with the force of the Holy Spirit all around him as he spoke these words into existence, "God will bring down your enemies and show His self mighty! You will not be at the bottom but at the top! Wait on God to do it! God is going to bring it all to you. You are not going to have to worry or make a decision. Wait!"

I asked him what to do about land we had just purchased. He looked at me and said, "Don't sell the land. Listen for God. Believe God will deliver the money for you and not doubt!"

I have to admit, several times we have had trouble with this. Fear and doubt have crept in, and we wondered if we really were in God's will when it has taken so long to see progress in this situation.

Then Fred stood up to pray over me. Jeanne stood in back of me with her hands on my back, and his hands were over my head. Jeanne's hands felt hot. I felt as if there were a rushing wind around me and my head was on fire, just like when the apostles were baptized in the Holy Ghost on Pentecost! Virtue descended upon me. Power. I cried. Fred prayed for prosperity and abundance and financial blessings to everything I touch and do. Peace.

When he finished praying he said, "How fast you believe is how fast it will come."

COME OUT OF HER MY PEOPLE
Part Two

When I quit and took all the charts I had been working on back to the office to turn them in, it was a bad scene. The office manager yelled at me in front of everyone. I was already sick with the flu and a 102 degree temperature. With her still yelling at me, I started praying out loud for the people and the business to go on without me. I was taking my hands off the business and let God do what He will. Then I left.

I then went to the local doctor's office where I helped out. I took them their files for their patients. I informed their office manager of what happened. She then informed me I was now once again their private patient assistance coordinator. And don't be late for work! I thanked her and asked if I could see the doctor for some medication.

All we had in the world by this time was $7.00 in the bank, two canned goods, a half jar of peanut butter and a sleeve of crackers. Ten years earlier I was in the same situation, no food when God came through. The doctor saw me and gave me some medicine out of his supply room. He told me to go to the store and get a $4.00 medication. We now had less than $3.00 in the bank.

On the way home I dropped off the last of the pamphlets to Community Services to help their clients in need. When I went in to give the ladies there the pamphlets I told Lynn, the lady in charge, a little of what happened. I told her I had medicine to take but I had no food to take it with. As a community resource could she please give me enough food to take my medicine? She jumped up from her desk hollering, "Emergency! Emergency! We have a family in urgent need!"

40

They stacked a grocery cart full with boxes and bags of groceries and toiletries. A series of miracles had started happening.

Mark couldn't believe all the food in the cabinets when he got home that evening. At 3 am that morning a good friend of ours, Pastor Ivie Dennis, was awakened and told to bring Mark a check for $75.00. The next night my mother was awakened and told to send us $50.00!

By that Friday our income tax return of $800.00 came in. Two weeks later our incentive from the government came in. In less than one month of obeying the Lord and letting Him take over, we had over $300.00 worth of groceries and $2,000.00 in the bank! Plus, another friend came and made a $635.00 payment for us!

You can't make this kind of stuff up! We were just along for a wonderful glorious ride! Everything Fred had prayed for us was falling right out of Heaven and onto our plate!

BORN AGAIN
Part One

Three days before our youngest son, Andy's 19th birthday, he was baptized in the Holy Spirit! The Holy Spirit fell on him and he began speaking in tongues. He was filled with joy! He was a new creation! Who could he call first to tell that would understand? Why Momma and Mark Dad of course! He talked to Mark for an hour and then he talked to me for an hour! He said to me, " Momma, I can see everything so clearly now!" We are all crying and thanking God. Then Andy called his big brothers to share his good news and talked to them for 1 ½ hours until they hung up on him because they wouldn't accept his message of salvation immediately!

That's okay son. Nazareth gave Jesus trouble too. What a wonderful Christmas present for all of us!

Bless God. Bless Andy.

When we saw him on Christmas Day he was still glowing!

BORN AGAIN
Part Two

Three months later, the Holy Spirit fell on Andy again, and he cried. It was the first time he had cried in many years. He forgave all the people who had ever injured him. He felt such peace and love surround him. He received a revelation from God. God is about love. He is love. When we love we are as close to God as "like God". When you lust, you are the least like God. It kind of puts all the world's problems into perspective, doesn't it?

42

A MIRACLE FOR MOMMA

I am known for volunteering my husband, Mark to help people in need. My dear friend of 27 years, Gail, told me she had a dilemma. They needed to move her son and his family back to Indiana from Texas, but they needed one more driver to go along. I immediately offered my husband for the four day trip. How could he ever thank me?

Two days before he was to leave town, we went to see his mom. She had been ill with a stomach flu. The stomach flu has a 48 hour incubation period, which is exactly what happened next.

At 5 am on the morning Mark was to leave for his trip, I was sitting in the bathroom crying , "Oh no! Not now!" There was nothing he could do about the circumstances. Mark was ready to walk out the door in one hour! He told me he would pray for me and would call me as he could. He got me some ginger ale and out the door he went.

When it got to be a decent hour in the day, shortly after noon, I started calling our sons to please bring me some more ginger ale or some chicken broth soup. I was too weak to get up. I called all three boys and left them messages. The first one that called me back was David, our middle son. He was at work and couldn't take off. He said he hoped I got better and he would say a prayer for me. I thanked him for calling me and at least seeing about me. I did not hear from our oldest son, Ben. [It turned out he was coming down sick and didn't want us to exchange germs! He had streph and mononucleosis at the same time. He ended up with us for eight days, between two different emergency room visits, until he was well enough to go home. So much for his good intentions. It was a nice try, Son.]

But the baby, Andy, (he hates it when I call him "the baby") called me back mid afternoon. He said, "Momma, I am going to take off early and come and bring you some ginger ale. I'll be there shortly." Happy Day! It worked out for one of them to come and help me! This is just one of the reasons you should be very good to your children and take care of them while they are growing up. It sets an example of what they should do for you!

Andy showed up at the house and brought in an eight pack of sprite. He came into the bedroom boldly announcing "Momma, I will not cook for you, but I will take you to dinner. We are meeting Tyler for dinner. Sleep for half an hour, and then we have to go." A half hour later I got out of bed, threw on sweat pants and a shirt and off we went!

We met Tyler, his best friend since 7th grade, at the restaurant. Tyler is easy to spot in a crowd. He is well over six feel tall, blond, and very Nordic looking. Smiling, he walked over for hugs. He is genuinely a nice young man.

I ordered a bowl of potato soup. I was only able to eat four or five bites but, the reason I could hardly eat was because I was laughing so hard at these two big goofs I was having dinner with! One story after another, bam, bam! All of their adventures came rolling out to cheer me up! They were laughing. I was laughing, and I thought, "Where was I when they were up to all these shenanigans? Holy cow!"

The evening came to an end, and Andy brought me home. He tucked me in bed and got me a glass of sprite and some crackers. Then he stood at the end of the bed for a minute thinking. He said to me, "Momma, you aren't sick. God didn't make you to be sick. He made you strong. I am leaving now. I have to go back to work and make up my time for leaving early. But, I am going before the Lord for you. I will let you know what He says." As he left, I nodded off to sleep. Twenty minutes later, the phone rang. It was Andy, and he had a reply from God for me. He had been before the Lord. This was what God had to say to our 19 year old son.

God said, "*I HAVE HEALED HER. WHY DOES SHE BELIEVE THE LIAR?"*

Instantly the fever, the nausea and lower bowel distress were gone! Just like a light switch being turned on, I went from darkness to light! I yelled into the phone, "I'm healed! I'm healed! Praise God! Thank you son!"
"Your welcome, Momma," he replied, "I love you! Bye!"

I got up and went and got my soup from the refrigerator, heated it up and ate heartily. I felt fine. I had tremendous energy flowing through my body. I watched the news. Mark called me and I told him what had happened. He said he had been praying for me. I said, "all prayers were answered."

Andy called to check on me at 10 pm that evening. I told him dinner stayed down just fine, I had talked to Mark and told him of our events, and now I was watching the news. He was very pleased I held onto my victory.

After the news, I settled down to read my bible for awhile. At 11:30 pm I got another call while I was still reading. I answered the phone and it was Andy again. He said, "Momma! Why are you still up? You need your sleep! Go to bed and get rest!"

Isn't it funny how roles of parent and child can reverse so quickly?

Laughing I promised him I would go right to bed!
"Much love, good son."
"Much love, good momma."

ALL THINGS ARE POSSIBLE

When I took over a patient assistance program in 2003 from our good friend and physician , I got to meet one of his patients, a man named Orville McClellen, "Mac" as he liked to be called, and his wife, Joyce. Finest kind. He related a story to me and asked me to tell as many people as I could. Well, surely I can.

Mac was a short, stocky, elderly old fashioned preacher man. His wife was petite in form but strong in character. They are a blended family. Joyce's first husband had died. Mac's first wife left him due to the inconvenience of a mentally challenged child.

Mac and Joyce had been together almost 20 years when he started having severe heart problems. The decision was made to do open heart surgery at a Louisville Hospital. Because of the complications of the surgery, the doctor's could not immediately close the incision in the chest cavity.

They wrapped bands around him until Mac was well enough to close the wound. Mac was encouraged to sit up on occasion to keep pneumonia from setting in his lungs. About the 18th day Joyce was sitting with Mac, and he didn't look well. He told her to go get a nurse. A large, male nurse named Rubin came in to help him lay back down into bed. This particular nurse had been called in on his day off. It was unusual for him to be there on that day. But Mac liked the man and was comforted to see him come into the room to assist him.

That's when Mac's aorta blew a hole in his heart the size of an egg. Blood went everywhere! Rubin immediately went into action! Shoving his massive hand deep into the open wound, he wrapped his hand around Mac's heart and stopped the free bleed out.

He started hollering for help!

Another small female nurse jumped up on top of Mac and started CPR to keep blood and oxygen flowing to his brain and vital organs. Two orderlies showed up and unhooked the bed from all the equipment and started flying down the hallway toward surgery.

Mac floated in and out. He tried to mumble, "Don't tell Momma." He was afraid for her and the children. His spirit kept rising up out of his body and coming back down. He would mumble and leave out again.

By the time they got him to surgery and the doctors and nurses were scrubbing up, Mac had fully left his body. His spirit was up on the ceiling watching all that was taking place. He turned to his left and saw Jesus there with him. Mac cried out for help, "Why me, Lord?"

Jesus calmly told him, *"**All things are possible to those that believe.**"*

Mac cried out a second time, "I believe, Lord! I believe!" Then Orville "Mac" McClellen slowly descended back into his body. He awoke several days later.

When he was good and alert, they called all the physicians together who were present at his surgery. With everyone's attention on Mac, the doctor's asked, "Who were you talking to in the operating room?" They had all witnessed something there, and they wanted an explanation. Mac gave his witness account. Shocked, now knowing he had an out of the body experience, they continued asking questions. "What did it feel like when you left your body?" Mac told them, "No pain, there was no pain."

They called him a "miracle man" at the hospital. He said, "No. I am the Miracle Man's son.

Orville McClellen was a very special man. God called him very young to the ministry. At eleven years old he was ordained a minister. He preached until he was 75, when he could get anyone to sit still long enough to witness to them the gospel truth.

I had the privilege of anointing twice and praying scripture over his wife, Joyce within 24 hours of her death. I kissed her and thanked her for all her wonderful years of service. I thanked her for her friendship.

Mac came to my home on a Tuesday and brought all his notes to join with mine. We had a wonderful time laughing and crying together. He stayed a good three hours with no problems breathing or getting around by himself.

On Thursday morning, November 4th, 2010, 38 hours after I had seen him, he went home to be with the Lord. We like to tell it this way. He sat down his coffee cup on the table with his breakfast, and God raptured him. When they found him less than an hour later, strangely enough, he looked twenty years younger.

Yes. He was raptured.

TWO "WARD" STORIES

When we met Jeremy and Holly Ward and their three children in 2008, I had no idea of the series of amazing events God would be leading us all to. These are some of their stories.

LUKE

Jeremy's son, Luke, was 17 years old. Jeremy helped his son get his first vehicle. He was allowed to drive back and forth to school, look for work and go on dates with his new girlfriend.

On the morning of the last day of school, Luke's step mother, Holly was on her way to work, and she felt a warning come on her to pray for Luke especially hard for his safety. She most assuredly did. Then Jeremy in the middle of his day, started getting the same message. He started praying for protection for his son as well.

Jeremy was in Kentucky in a clients's car when the call came through. It was Luke. He had been in a bad accident. Please come home right away! The police and ambulance were on their way! Jeremy called Holly, Pastor Schuppert and our home to call out for prayers.

We met them at the local hospital. They had pictures of the smashed truck on their cell phones. It was demolished alright! We waited to hear word on Luke and his girlfriend. The physicians in the emergency room x-rayed and checked them both out thoroughly. Luke had no broken bones or lacerations. He was shook up and sore. That's all. His girlfriend had a cut on her head. No trauma or concussion. In other words they were just fine.

Prayers were answered. Everyone was safe due to obedient parents that prayed for their son when the Holy Spirit prompted them.

Thank God.

MISS PAYTON

We have been very blessed by the Ward family being in our lives. They have three children named Luke, Shelby who was eight years old, and Miss Payton, who was five years old. God is the center core in all their lives.

The worst testing a parent can have is when their children get sick. Everything from the flu to cancer and all in between, parents just feel a mess inside until that child is well and on the mend. In the middle of the child being sick, you'd call out to anyone you thought could help, like the time we were called on the first Sunday morning in November of 2010.

The night before I had an allergic reaction to something I had bought at a bake sale earlier that day. I had to take Benadryl, which normally is not a problem, unless, you had a glass of wine, too while watching a movie with your husband. I got mighty sick, awfully quick. We prayed through it into the night. Mark was in bed singing to God on my behalf while I was in the bathroom. By the morning, all was done but the shouting. Glory!

We were just settling down to breakfast when the phone rang. The first words I heard from Holly were, "Thank God! Thank God you're home!" She had our attention right away! Mark stopped eating. Alarmed, I said, "What's wrong?" Holly related the story, "I need help. I'm at work. Payton is sick. Jeremy doesn't want to take her and Shelby out to the store. We need Children's Tylenol and children suppositories for constipation. Payton has been hurting for five days. I felt her abdomen and she feels like she is impacted on her right side. She hasn't had a bowel movement for days and her fever is going higher. Can you go to the store for us?"

51

"You bet, we're on it! We can leave here in a few minutes. Tell Jeremy to hang on, we can be there in a half hour! Love you," I say as I'm hanging up the phone.

I told my husband what was going on as we scurried into clothes and got out the door. Breakfast was left on the kitchen table. We ran in the drug store and bought the requested medications. We arrived at their home twenty minutes later.

Jeremy and Payton were on the couch. We hugged Jeremy. He looked happy to see us. The first thing he told us was he knew we were praying for Payton because she stopped crying and her pain was much better. Jeremy relayed to us what had been going on the last week. Payton had trouble with her bowels locking up. She's had a fever off and on. I got her something to drink, her Tylenol and the suppository.

I explained to her what a suppository is and what it does. I asked her if she would allow me to help her. She said okay. The men stayed in the kitchen making coffee until it was over. She took her Tylenol and sips of drinks for me. Holly called every ten minutes asking for a report.

Once all the medicine had time to work, her temperature started coming down and she was cleaning out nicely as the men went once again into the kitchen and shouted encouragement to us in the bathroom! Payton's eyes brightened as she felt better and could easily sit up on her own. We knew she would be fine when she started asking for food and drink. Then she wanted to play with her sister.

When we left that afternoon at 2 pm we felt she was on the mend. We talked to the family a couple of times during the week. Payton's temperature kept spiking over and over. Finally, by mid-week, Holly took her to the doctor. He diagnosed her with streph and gave her an antibiotic. Holly started her on it that afternoon.

Still, something was not right. Payton was not reacting right. Jeremy and Holly called Pastor Fred for prayers.

One evening, God called out to Holly in a dream. He told her, *"I have healed her. Not the medicine. It is the wrong antibiotic."*

Within three days Holly got confirmation of this. The doctors office called and said it was the wrong medicine to give to her, it was strain resistant. The doctor offered to call in a new medication. Holly gave her witness report to the nurse on the other end of the telephone line. The office called in the prescription just in case.

The Ward family showed up the next week for church. Everyone was right as rain. The reign of God, that is.

GAIL

I would like to introduce Gail to you. We have known each other for half of our lives, twenty-six years for you mathematicians. I am not sure how to put someone larger than life on paper, but I will give it a try.

When she was born, her cry was so long and so loud her father named her Gail, as in a strong wind. As she grew, that strong wind got much stronger in character, voice and in spirit.

In her family, there are generation after generation of preachers of which her father, Paul, is one. This sweet generous man has danced before the Lord, filled with the Holy Spirit. At 86 years young, he is officially retired. Their family is closely guarded by angels with many miracles that one could document. I will name a few here.

Gail has been everything from my very best friend to **"<u>not!</u>"** my best friend! We both have very wise husbands who stay out of the latter part of that sentence. We have been big helps to each other and our families are closely knit. If one is in the thick of something, the other is probably right along with them. We have six boys and one girl between our families.

Gail is well on her way to spoiling her fourteen grandchildren.

I informed her I am not through spoiling my children, yet!

These next three stories are hers.

Enjoy.

EASTER SUNDAY MIRACLE

Gail comes from a large vibrant family. They hold get togethers from Ohio to Indiana. At one of these gatherings in rural southern Indiana were her brother, Daniel and his son Danny, along with cousins and a lot of other people. Danny and Chase went four wheeling on a neighbor's property. Danny hit a rut and flipped the jeep. He was thrown out and called for Chase. Chase did not respond. He could not find him in the wreckage. Danny ran up to the house and got other family members. They jumped in other jeeps, went down to the area where the accident happened and flipped the jeep back over. There lay Chase. He was grey and blue with no respirations. Danny started CPR.

They called an ambulance who had him STAT flighted to a Louisville hospital. At the hospital, Chase died three more times. The doctors put him in a coma to help stabilize his condition. He had two collapsed lungs, a damaged spleen, head and neck trauma.

The family called out for prayer. We were notified to start praying about 11 pm that evening. Family members went to the hospital. When they were allowed into his room, they prayed over him. The machines around him started to respond!

On the third day, on Easter Sunday morning, he started waking up by himself! The hospital called it an Easter Sunday Miracle.

When there is no hope in man's eyes, there is hope in Jesus.

ANGEL OVER US

The way I became related to Gail was by marriage. We married cousins. Except after 15 years, I was no longer married to her husband's cousin. The decision was made then to keep each other.

In 1989, Gail and Mike had been married for over eight years. Mike was in trouble with alcohol. They had four children together.

One evening, several unusual occurrences were happening in their home. Bad things. Their son, Michael, then eight years old, saw a gremlin coming in and out of his room and he couldn't sleep. Their son, Kaelin saw shadows going across his door. And lastly, her husband, Mike, was seeing black things flying around him in the room!

By this time Gail had enough! She told her husband to go lay down and she would be with him shortly.

Gail called her mother and told her what was going on in their house! Both women started praying together. Gail went back to the bedroom and laid down with Mike. She started praying over him. The Holy Spirit fell, and she started singing and praying in tongues. Then Gail looked up and saw an angel over her house. It was a man dressed in armor! He stood 30 feet tall. That's when she realized she could see through her roof! She wanted Mike to see it, but he had fallen asleep. When she went to wake him, the angel left.

Gail got up and called her mom. When Hazel answered the phone, Gail told her what had happened. Her mother then told Gail that she had been praying for God to send an angel over her house!

All the occurrences stopped.
Mike stopped drinking and gave his heart to God.

HAZEL

Gail's mother's name was Hazel. Hazel passed away Christmas Eve of 2006. Gail and her dad, Paul, were with her in her home when she died. Even though Gail saw her mother die peacefully, Gail had no peace. She wanted to talk to her mother just one more time.

Thanksgiving time rolled around the first year. Gail's father, Paul got a phone call from his son Richard in Ohio. Then Paul called Gail, who in turn called us crying. She had a story to tell.

Her niece Mary Ann worked at a hospital in Ohio. The weirdest thing had happened at work a few night ago. They thought the rest of the family needed to know. Mary Ann had gone to work the night shift. She had forgotten something in her car and went out to retrieve it. When she turned around to go back to the hospital, there was an older man standing next to her.

He said to her, "I have something I need to tell you." She said, "Oh no, I have to go back to work." He continued, "No, I have to tell you a message from Hazel. Hazel is jumping up and down trying to get my attention. Hazel said to tell your daddy she is fine now. She is sorry she died on Christmas. She wants all of you to stop crying and have a happy Christmas." Then he talked about two old deceased aunts of Mary Ann's to confirm for her that this message really was for her family.

She went back into the hospital, went upstairs and immediately called her dad. She told him everything. He then called his father down in Indiana and told him.

What is the reason God sent an angel to the people in Ohio? That was the part of the family that had not accepted God or Jesus. From Heaven, Hazel was still trying to save family members left here! What a Momma! This confirms for me that we do still have our family in heaven. We will know each other. And pray for each other!

TEETH

The fall of 2010 was a very good time for our family. Out of seven of us, four were starting great new jobs. The other three already had great jobs. This is a wonderful thing to have happen to a family while the rest of the economy is crying out about job losses and unemployment skyrocketing!

Thank you God, that You delivered us from these times.

At the same time, there was a rash of tooth aches occurring on many people we knew including myself. At the end of November, I had to have a root canal. God was with me. There was blood in the canal but no active infection. The dentist caught it just in time! Dr. Randy will see Mark and I December 13 for a full dental cleaning and check up.

A few days later, a church family member came over for lunch and a visit with her four children. In the middle of eating lunch, the middle of one of my teeth fell out onto my plate. Lisa asked, "What's that? It looks like your tooth!" I ran to the bathroom, got out a small flashlight and looked. I had Lisa look too. The middle of one of my teeth had fallen out. I could see pink gum around the area. I knew this was not good.

When my husband got home from work, I had him look. He saw the same thing! In my heart I thought, "Oh no! Where will we get another $2,000.00 for this?" I cried. My husband almost cried.

We went to church that evening and I told everyone what happened. I asked Pastor Fred to pray over me. He prayed hard and stood firm. Afterwards he said he didn't know what had come over him. He had never prayed with so much zeal for something like that before.

He felt he was supposed to do it. I received every word he uttered. I felt power come down from the Heavens.

The next morning I got up and went to see my miracle. There it was. There was tooth again where there had been a hole. I started laughing and praising! I showed Mark. He started yelling "Praise the Lord!" I called our pastor's home and gave our witness report to his wife Jeanne.

I went to the dentist two days later. All it needed was a filling. No root canal or cap. No blood or infection. Two hundred dollars, thanks.

You bet! Glory!

ANGELIC VISITATIONS

"The angel of the Lord encampeth round about them that fear Him, and delivereth them."
                                        Psalm   34:7

"For He shall give His angels charge over thee, to keep thee in all thy ways. They shall bear thee up in their hands, lest thou dash thy foot against a stone."
                                        Psalm 91:11-12

PROLOGUE

There have been times in my life when God has sent angels to show me something, speak to me a word of knowledge out loud, minister to me, or take me up in the spirit. When I am in the spirit, or taken away, there is no breathing, no pain, no heaviness of the body. There is no feeling at all.

I have been awake, and I have been asleep. Standing or sitting it makes no difference. There is no time frame, it can be past events, future events, mostly it has been in the heavens with heavenly information being received.

All the angels I have ever seen are much larger than people. I have not yet been given a name for any of them. They have all been "helpers" to me. So that's what I tend to call them, my helpers.

Their look was of the heavenly realm, with whiter than our natural white arraiments on.

There are five parts to this so far!

OUT OF BODY EXPERIENCES

HEAVEN
Part One

I was taken up in the spirit to what I would call the heavenly realm or space. I was with an angel. Sitting before us was the Book of Life. They pointed to a page and I could see my name written there. I knew it was me! The spelling was:

"Debbie Aubrie" I leapt for joy!

"I made it!" I cried! I started turning the massive pages and said to the angel, "I want to go to the "M's" to see if my boys make it."

Then I was back in the flesh.

VERIFICATION

After this "first of a kind dream" I had, on my next birthday, I received a gift from my friends in England. They traced my name back to its origin. In 14th century Wales, the spelling of my last name was "Aubrie".

HEAVEN
Part Two

Later, that same night, I was again taken up in the spirit. This was a very active night! I was taken into the sky over land I did not recognize. I asked the angel, "What is this?" The angel replied, "When you see this land, you will know what it is. The last battle will be fought here."

I was not afraid. I had no trouble breathing. It was as if I recognized this as supernatural. Knowledge was given.

VERIFICATION

The next year before my brother, Ron, got out of the military, he was in the Middle East. We received pictures of the "good ole Kentucky boy" sitting on a camel by the pyramids. He was all over the area. When he came home to visit he brought many more pictures with him. I was looking at them when I came to one I recognized.

I told Ron about the dreams I had been having over the course of time. The land I was shown by the angel was the picture he was showing me then. I asked him, "Where is this?" He looked at me with wide eyes and said, "That's Israel, Deb. It's Megiddo Valley." I said, "Armageddon". His reply to me was, "One day, we will know what planet you are really from."

66

HEAVEN
Part Three

By the time of the next dream, I was married to Mark. Lying in bed peacefully asleep, an angel came again and took me up into space, high above the earth. It was not Heaven, it was space around the earth. I was not afraid, or cold or gasping for air. I looked down.

The angel said, "It happens now. Armageddon is now."

I could see people fighting. Everywhere I looked I saw good and evil fighting. It was all over the earth. God's Holy people were in white and glowing. Evil was dark and ugly. They were very frightening to look at.

INTERPRETATION

Armageddon is now. It is going on now. On our streets, in our towns, in ourselves. It is everywhere hate exists. If hate is in our hearts, it exists there. This is the war! It is internal and external. Don't wait for the last battle to begin to get involved. The war has already started.

To win the battle outside, we must win the battle inside. LET GO.

You know what I mean. If I can do it, you can too. LET GO.

That's when God takes over and His battle for good begins.

HEAVEN

Part Four

I was taken up to Heaven again by an angel. I could see a long line of people. Everyone who had ever been born was in line. All those who were truly in Christ, lived their faith, convicted in Him, our Lord came and held their hand. He said to His Father, "This one is mine Father."

Glory!!!

HEAVEN
Part Five

The last time I was taken up into the heavenly realm by an angel was in 2008. I saw many people I knew who had passed. I asked the angel if this was Heaven. He said to me, "This is the garden, a pleasant place to wait for the final judgment." Happiness and joy filled the air. Peace, understanding and knowledge were prevalent in my being and all around me. I was filled with joy! Once I could take this all in I was immediately transported to the other place.

This was a dark place of mourning. You could feel malice in the air. The feeling there was of dense disturbance. I asked the angel to please take me from this place because I was very frightened!

Immediately I was shown the Great Judgment. I was in line too. People were placing their crowns and jewels before Christ. This was a representation of all the good and love they had done in their lives for Yeshua the King.

There were two different lines; two different judgment seats, the Great White Throne Judgment and the Judgment Seat of Christ.

My last memory in that dream was looking at the jewels in my arms and wondering if that was enough to get in Jesus's line. Then I awoke.

I will say this for any of you out there reading this and for myself:
If you are in the line with jewels in your arms to set before Christ, you are in the line of the Judgment seat of Christ and not the Great White Throne Judgment!
DON'T BE AFRAID!!

Angelic Visitations

ANGELS ALL AROUND ME!

One day, when my youngest son Andy, was six years old, we were walking up the stairs in our townhouse apartment. He turned to me and said, "Mommy, there are angels all around you." He smiled so beautiful I knew he must have been seeing them.

Without missing a beat I replied, "It figures, it would take more than one guardian angel for me!"

As a Catholic, I was taught everyone only had one angel each. But out of my baby's mouth came revelation. If he said we have more, I believe him because he believes God.

VERIFICATION

The summer of my 52nd year (in 2010), in the evening, my husband and I were out shopping in Clarksville, Indiana. We were getting low on gasoline and pulled over to a gas station to fill up. While my husband was pumping gas, I walked into the store to buy something. My turn in line came up and the lady looked like she didn't feel very well. Automatically I asked her if she needed prayer. She brightened up and said yes! I prayed a simple prayer of healing over her. When I was finished she looked up at me and said, "Do you know you have angels all around you?"

Yes, I know. Do you know you have angels all around you to be at your beck and call because God loves you so? Why don't you thank Him right now?

Put the book down right now, and go before God to tell Him how awesome He is! How wonderful it is to have Him in your life! Thank Him for Jesus as our savior, example and way home. And keep a log of all the miracles in your life.

AN ANGEL IN FLORIDA

In 1992, I was still married to my first husband. We were living in Indiana. Our youngest son was 2 ½ years old, followed by four year old David, and seven year old Benjamin. Clarence had family that lived in Florida, and we thought it would be nice to go for a visit. Everything went fine on the way down. The visit was pleasant and so was the weather. We took the boys to the beach several days and out sightseeing on other days.

One of the days we went out sightseeing, we came across a little flea market. We put the babies in the double stroller, a back pack on Ben and went looking for fun! We got drinks and snacks, everyone got a little something to take home with them.

We started to walk past a small booth when Clarence stopped. It held very little in it. A counter, a table with a couple of chairs. Very sparse. No wares. A simple sign read, "$15.00 readings." Clarence said, "You should do this, Deb. I'll take the boys outside to play while we wait."

I walked over and said hello to a beautiful tall blond lady with a dazzling smile. She was wearing all white and had a very calming presence about her. "Please," she said, "Come and sit at the table with me."

She gave me paper to write down everything she was going to say. She asked me not to confirm anything she said, just to be quiet, listen, and write.

She asked if I had anything that she could hold to "see" with. I pulled my wedding rings out of my wallet change pocket and handed them to her. Holding them in her hands, she rolled the pieces back and forth between her fingers, she began to speak and I began to write.

Smiling, she said, "You have the heart of the Lamb. Gentle. Kind. Good.

71

You will be getting a new vehicle when you go home."

She went on, "You have children. A boy. The first one is you! He has the heart of the Lamb as well!" She was smiling. "You have another boy." Now she was laughing! "He goes where angels dare not tread! He is fearless!" Well, he is David, the Lionhearted! And he is! Then she stopped and looked puzzled and listened to a voice I could not hear. She spoke again, "Only two children were planned. You were only supposed to have two. But you have another boy. I can't read him as well. I don't understand." She looked truly puzzled as if this did not happen to her very often. "He is ill, or has been very ill. He won't be able to go and play like the others." He was still on breathing treatments from having Bronchialitis with RSV complications as a two month old baby. That is when he died and came back twice.

She stated, "Enjoy him while you have him. I am not seeing an extended life." That's the day I started praying long life over Andy!

I asked her to tell me about my husband. Her face darkened. Her breathing quickened. She told what she saw, "Darkness, darkness all around him. I don't like to read the dark places. He listens to the lower levels. From the depths, deep. He is disturbed. There are demonic influences."

I saw a disturbance on her face, close to panic. She said, "You are not safe there! You have to get out! Because of your caring heart, you have a medical aptitude you are not aware of. Go into a specialty like respiratory. Your stomach is too sensitive to work with blood. You must hurry!" She could see danger before me.

I tried to pay her but she wouldn't take any money. She hugged me and looked deep into my eyes. The last thing she said to me was, "I love you."

We had connected spirit to spirit.

I walked out into the daylight. The children were playing in the grass. I knew in my heart, from then on, things were going to be very different.

We went back the next day with his sister. I wanted Clarence's sister to meet her. We went back to where we thought her space was, and it was empty. I went looking for the manager of the flea market. I told him what had happened there yesterday and what the lady looked like. I asked, "Could you please direct me to her proper spot?"

He said he didn't remember anyone like that in his market. He thought we were confused about where we had been the day before. I insisted, "No! This is where we were yesterday!" We took him over to the space where we thought she had been. He turned to us and said, "This space has never been rented." He walked away.

Clarence and I looked at each other with our jaws dropped.

At that point, I knew she must have been an angel.

TWO PRAYERS AND AN ANGEL
Part One

In February of 2007, our oldest son, Ben, was in a bad place in his heart and spirit. He was bottoming out. He and his girlfriend of three years had broken up the day before. He tore up his car pretty good on purpose. The last of his money to pay end of the month bills was in danger of being flitted away.

That morning, Ben went out to his car and there were these two cards on his windshield. An angel had come by:

St. Augustine's Prayer

God of our life, there are days when the burdens we carry chafe our shoulders and weigh us down; When the road seems dreary and endless, the skies gray and threatening; When our lives have no music in them, and our hearts are lonely, and our souls have lost their courage.

Flood the path with light, turn our eyes to where the skies are full of promise; Tune our hearts to brave music; give us the sense of comradeship with heroes and saints of every age; And so quicken our spirits that we may be able to encourage the souls of all who journey with us on the road of life, to your honor and glory.

Do It Now!

I expect to pass through this world but once, Any good thing, therefore, that I can do or any kindness I can show to any fellow human being let me do it now!

Let me not defer nor neglect it; for I shall not pass this way again.

– Stephen Grellet

74

Ben called all around asking who had done this kindness, and no one confessed to it. But, it brought him out of the dark place he was in.

He decided to live again.

Thank you, unknown angel!

TWO PRAYERS AND AN ANGEL
Part Two
The rest of the story!

Years went by. Ben cleaned up his act, along with his younger brother, David. We are all very proud of both of them. They have both decided to live!

My husband Mark and I were on our way over to Ben's for a New Year's Eve party. While we were waiting for 2010 to turn into 2011, Ben told us this story.

"Momma, do you remember shortly after great Aunt Alma died, when I had my meltdown, and someone left the two cards on my windshield?"

"Yes, son."

He went on to inform me, "I found out who it was that left them. It was Dad."

"Really?!" I responded.

"Yeah. He said that Aunt Alma had come to him and told him he needed to give these cards to me. So he did."

"Wow."

Thank you Alma!
Thank you Clarence!
Thank you God!

INTERMISSIONS

WISDOM

Quote from Joan: "Be careful what you speak.
How many times have we chosen
Death in our lives with our
words?"

By what we speak, we are calling forth to the natural.
Do you want to give life to life, or life to death?
The Bible says we have a choice, choose life or death.
We need to train our minds, our eyes, our ears and our
hearts to hear, see and feel the difference.
These are all battlegrounds.
Once we realize that, we can choose more wisely.
If we have to live with that choice forever,
forever is a long time.

JOHN

In my 25th year, in between my first two miscarriages, and the twins I carried in my 26th year, I had a dream about another baby.

I dreamed I had a beautiful baby boy with dark hair. I named him John. Someone kidnapped him, and I went to look for him. I could hear him crying and screaming. I found him. He was crucified on a cross, and I couldn't reach him. I cried at the foot of the cross.

This could've been a warning that my children were going to suffer. I was in an abusive marriage for 15 years. My boys suffered as well even after we got out and the marriage was over. Post Traumatic Stress without God's divine intervention and healing can take a life time of therapy and medication to do it on your own.

In my 52nd year, while getting ready to write this book, I had a quick vision. It was maybe three to four seconds long. When I see visions there is nothing else. No sights or sounds or smells of where I should be.

Again I was at the foot of the cross, dressed in mourning attire for the first century Palestine. I was on the ground on my knees, looking across from me was Jesus. He had just been nailed to the cross. He was face down with the cross on top of him as they bent the nails into the wood so they couldn't be pulled out. The Roman soldiers had not yet pulled the cross up into position.

Jesus, Yeshua, turned his head and looked at me. He locked eyes with me. I did not see fear or pain in his eyes. I saw determination. He was determined. And I knew it was all for me.

And for you.

For everyone.

Then the vision was gone.

GOD THROUGH BEN'S EYES
BY   PAUL   BENJAMIN EARL MERK

We are the dreams of a sleeping God, a patchwork of hopes, joys, nightmares and fears. Our world sprang forth as his longing for companionship unfolded in the restless dreaming of his slumbering subconscious.

God is the living spirit. His presence is felt in the core of all living things. From the greatest peaks of life to the lowest piece of grass which grows in the light, the power of God is present. All things which exist God exists within. My spirit is but a drop of that infinite and intangible ocean which is God. My body and all bodies are his desires made flesh and all life are his hopes made good.

In the spirit of the world we are made in his image. Life begets unto life. For as God creates so must we. And as God has created and followed his own dream so must we. As every flower which gives its pollen to breed new life is working to do the will of God, so are we all.

God is embodied by a careful love which is tempered with the full range of emotions. When the storms clap loudly, God's awesome rage is felt most purely, although the storm may be the very cause of the spring flowers. God resides within the seasons and his ageless face can be seen painted across the rocks and deserts and flora and fauna of his vast and ever changing world.

He takes loving care in tending to the details which have allowed life to exist. He is an artist and a chemist, we are his living canvas. He breathes life across the borders and shades the background until pure. As living works of art God gives us the opportunity to paint ourselves. Who we are is a product of where we were; and all that together with God's will creates who we will become.

God, like an imaginative child, has grown as time has moved onward. The clumsiness of a child's finger painting has given way to the skill of a trained artist. All life springs forth from God and all life is inseparable from God. Like raindrops we fall as spirits made flesh. All we think, feel, and experience shall be returned to God. We make God more full, more whole, and we fulfill the purpose of Gods desire to know himself in all his many facets. Again I say, all life flows forth from God and all life shall be returned unto God.

The value and purpose of subjective good and evil are but a mirror for one another. For what is passion without its lesser? And is a passions opposite its lesser or is it more truly an unrivaled equal. For in the heart of God there are a million shades of black and white and gray, but without the furthest reaches of a spectrum could the in between be known?

God is passion and resides within the deepest part of our hearts. When drawn to create with words, or music, or art, or love, then the heart of God is expressed in our works. When we follow our passions, and not the petty worries which life presents, then God smiles upon our faces. His light shines out and touches our souls and for a moment, when following passions, our souls can touch upon the infinite.

Part Two

WALKING IN THE SUPERNATURAL

"Call unto me, and I will answer thee, and shew thee great and mighty things, which thou knowest not."
Jer. 33:3

PROLOGUE

I am going to try to explain supernatural events with natural language and its limitations. In some stories there will be a shift in a story that I don't have the physical words for. I will do my best to guide readers as close to these experiences as the English language will allow. Thank you for understanding.

In my lifetime I have seen colors that could not be experienced by the naked eye. I have seen the lack of color when death is approaching. Everything I see is in black and white and grey.

I have smelled death on people. It smells of rotten eggs. It's the loosening of the spirit from the body. For the body without the breadth of God in it is dead and rotten flesh. I have smelled it over a baby once and the elderly several times.

Our son, Andy, smells when " good" is going to happen to people. It smells sweet to him. I am waiting for him to smell it on me!

I have seen, felt, and heard in the spirit and outside my head, angels many times. Once, I have heard Yeshua. "Call me Yeshi, thanks." Friends.

And once I heard the voice of God out of rolling thunder. These are all stories forth coming.

I have seen the Shekinah Glory of God over a priest at a healing service.

I have felt healing on my body many times and seen it on others as well.

I cannot explain these occurrences in the natural world, only in the supernatural. I guess that's where I walk.

AURAS

Aura – An invisible emanation
aureole – a halo
emanation– to come forth, issue, as from a source

Colors–
Green– healing, harvest
Blue– peace and tranquility
Yellow– Glory of God
Black– death

I name these specific colors because these are the only ones I have seen personally. I have seen aura's around people, and things like in books, especially highlighting in the Bible. My husband's new truck has a blue aura.

I wonder if that is why we are drawn to certain people or things. For example, when we all say things like, "Oh, that is just perfect! It is just what I have been looking for!" Or you are drawn to certain people. Maybe there is an aura around them that only your spirit eyes can see. That is a confirmation for you. After all, we don't believe in coincidence! You have peace about buying something before laying down hard earned money, or when you automatically like someone you have just met.

Highlighting in books happens to my husband and I frequently. The color yellow emanates from the bible for us. To me, this is God's way of talking to me while I am searching out His word.

My experiences with aura's can be found in some of the following stories.

FAMILY

I like to think our family is just like ever other family in America. We go to work, raise our children, pay our mortgages and bills, some go to church, everyday life. At family gatherings, we talk, laugh, and sometimes disagree. And sometimes as evenings wind down, stories are whispered about things not easily explained. These are a few of those.

When my oldest brother was living in an apartment with his wife early in their marriage, he woke up to find our Dad sitting at the end of his bed. Dad was there to warn Jack they had to get up and move! Someone was coming to kill him! Jack heeded Dad's words and moved in short order. He thought it nothing unusual that Dad had come to warn him. After all, that's what a good father does. He looks out for his children. He saved their lives. At the time, Dad had been deceased for several years.

My mother has always had a strong instinct for when something was wrong, or when miracles were happening. Like the time her own dear father was dying. He passed away at 5:30am at the hospital. Momma got up crying because he had come to tell her good by. At 6 am she got a call confirming what she already knew.

In our family there are "big brother" and "big sister" and "little sister" and "little brother". My brother Ron and I are little brother and little sister. Ron and I have been close ever since he was big enough to wop me in the nose. He let me know we were now on equal ground and I couldn't push him around anymore. Instant best friends ever since. We were eight and nine years old respectively.

88

When he became of age, he went into the navy. He did his 20 year stint, and at the age of 42, he retired. He came home with a new wife, Devin, ready to start his next career. In the meantime, while still looking for work, Ron did maintenance and clean up work for our sister Vicki who was in the real estate field.

It was in the middle of the summer and the day's heat was up in the 90's when Vicki asked Ron to paint the inside of a house for her. He was to get it ready to go on the real estate market. The air conditioner was turned off in the house because no one was living there at the time. The elderly lady who had lived there had recently passed away. This was to be a part of an estate sale.

While in the home he felt as if someone was watching him from the top of the stairs, but when he looked no one was there. Later, while he was painting, he walked past a window. It was so cold as he walked past it on this 90 degree day that he could see his breath! Cold as ice! Just like in the movies! Ron put down his paint brush and went out the door. He locked up the house. Then he went to the nearest Kroger and bought flowers.

Ron came back to the house, unlocked the kitchen door, and put the flowers on the kitchen table. Then he called out, "I know this is your home. I am just here to paint the walls so your home will look nice and new again! See, I brought you flowers!"

"After all," he reasoned, "all women like flowers." Such a classy man! He had no more problems.

You see, God made energy, life, as everlasting, just like Himself. He welcomes us to come back to Him at the end of our days here. He even made it easy for us by sending His Son Jesus to show us the way back home. By the shedding of Jesus' blood, covered under His blood, we can all go home again.

How do we thank God, Jesus, for this? With our voice, our heart, our actions, our faith, with our life.

UNCLE PAUL

The day after Thanksgiving in the year 2010 was a busy one. The women in our family were preparing to go "Black Friday" shopping! The men in our family were not! Well, at least, Uncle Paul was happy to stay at Momma's house and put up some Christmas decorations with my brother Ron.

We headed out to several malls. We people watched and bargain hunted. We only had a fixed amount of time because my sister Vicki was helping our youngest son in finding and buying a home. And later, there was going to be a family dinner to celebrate a birthday! There was so much to do in one day!

We finally arrived back at Momma's later in the afternoon. Vicki went home to cook. Momma and Aunt Marilyn went into the living room to have a cigarette. I stayed in the kitchen with Uncle Paul. I told him of our day's events.

As we were talking and waiting for the time to come to go to Vicki's for dinner, Uncle Paul related stories to me. He told me of his daughter Karen, and their last baby, Blessing. When she was born she had several things wrong with her, especially her eyes. Uncle Paul knew she would be alright and that her eyes would clear up by the next week with no explanation. He knew that the doctors would verify this to Karen. It happened exactly as Uncle Paul had foretold.

After telling me this story, he looked up at me and said, "I have known things all my life. I just know that sooner or later all things told to me will come to pass. Can you understand this?"

Perfectly, Uncle Paul. Perfectly.

HELP!

I have heard many times in my life, for lack of a better word, a "guardian angel" speak. It has always been a male voice, out loud, outside of my head. It has brought warnings, healing or healing words, instructions, whatever was necessary at the time.

The first time I can remember a clairaudient event, I was about nine years old. I was at a friend's house down in her basement watching television with her after school. I heard, *"Go upstairs now!"*. It was a command!

I jumped up and ran upstairs. Her mother, Kathleen, was sitting on the phone and couldn't get off. Her skillet was about to catch fire! She said, "Debbie, pull that skillet off the stove!" I grabbed a potholder and moved the skillet to the side.

Then I went back downstairs to watch TV again with Karen. She asked me where I went. I replied her mother needed my help upstairs. She then asked me how I knew, but by that time I was already engrossed in our afternoon soap opera.

MY AURA

When I first met Clarence, my first husband, in 1979, one of the first things he said to me was "there is a white aura all around you." At the time I had no idea what an aura was or what it meant to have one.

When I was 46 years old, a nurse I knew came up to me, smiled and said, "You have a beautiful blue aura." Blue auras, according to her, are associated with speech, communication skills, written and verbal.
Of course.
God equips His saints.

Have you taken stock of your equipment?

Maybe you should.

DADDY

Six months after I married Clarence, when I was 21 years old, my father, Earl, became very ill. The doctors put him in a local hospital in Louisville, Kentucky. On Good Friday morning they were going to do exploratory surgery.

I woke up early that morning and all the color was gone from my sight. I could only see black, white, and grey. I knew in my heart that this meant bad news for my Daddy.

After surgery that afternoon the surgeon came in the room and announced to the family that daddy had cancer of the liver, and it was so advanced it was terminal. He had two months to live. He died three months later.

What I want you to understand here is, that God did not change the circumstances, He prepared me for them.

During this time Clarence was transferred with Red Barn to Omaha, Nebraska. One evening in July, I could feel my daddy near by. I knew if I saw him he would die that night. I told Clarence to turn on all the lights, I did not want to see my daddy!

My mother told me when I flew home the next week to see them, that Dad had been hallucinating. He told her that he could hear me in the other room last week. He wanted to know why didn't I come in and see him. I do not think he was hallucinating.

1984

Have you ever had a warning you felt coming a good portion of your life? Well, it sort of goes like this....

I was raised in the '60's and the '70's. George Orwell was a big writer at the time, and he wrote the book "1984". Man! I had a dread about that year even though I never did read the book. I didn't know what it was, but I knew it was fearful deep down in my heart.

The Christmas of 1983, I was six weeks pregnant with my second pregnancy. My first one had ended in a miscarriage. My husband at the time, Clarence, bought the new baby several gifts. One was a teddy bear candle that had written on it's shirt, "God Bless". I still have the candle to this day, 27 years later.

Christmas went very well. December 28th did not. I went into work not feeling well due to morning sickness. Clarence dropped me off at work. Later that afternoon I got a call from our local fire department telling me that there had been a fire at my house. I needed to meet them there. A friend from work took me back to our home and dropped me off. I met the fire chief, and he explained how he thought the accident happened. I signed his statement, and he left me there.

It was bitterly cold outside and I had no vehicle to go anywhere. I went into the house shell, closed the door and sat on a wet burned out couch. I was young, pregnant and in shock. After a few minutes, I heard a knock on the kitchen door. It was two of my neighbors. I was in such shock that all I could think to say was, "I'm sorry. We have had a fire and I don't have anywhere for you to sit." They took me to their home, gave me fresh clothes to wear, and put me to bed.

When Clarence got home from work, he found me at the neighbors home. He contacted our insurance company, and they put us up at a Holiday Inn until they could get us an apartment. I felt things were going to get a lot worse.

On December 31, 1983, I got on my knees and prayed very hard, "God please let this cup pass me by. I do not want to drink of it." I could feel it coming and had no way of stopping it.

Sometimes God gives us warning dreams to prepare us for what we are about to go through. Unfortunately we can't always pray away situations. We just have to hold on tight and trust God to see us through it all.

By the second week of January, 1984, the insurance company had us an apartment. They sent us to a store to rent all the furniture we would need. They settled funds with Clarence two weeks later.

During this time I had a warning dream, that satan came and took my baby from my belly. Then he raped me while I was still bleeding. The next morning I woke up bleeding from my nose and my vagina.

Within seven days I was admitted to the hospital for a three day stay. The baby had died in uterus, and the doctor had to do a D&C. When I came back home from the hospital, Clarence took off to get the insurance checks.

Two days later, an acquaintance of Clarence's came to the apartment. He drug me by the hair of my head into my bedroom, beat my head against the head board, and while still bleeding from my miscarriage, he raped me.

The whole dream had come true with a vengeance.

I don't have any wisdom, or reason for this.

I was not told why it would happen, only that it would.

Have mercy on me oh Lord, have mercy.

HEALING

After the incident of the rape, I carried pain in my heart for several years. I was afraid satan was going to take my soul to hell. I was being punished.

God is so merciful. He sent a lovely lady to tell me I was not intended for hell but Heaven! Imagine my relief! I believed her then and I believe her now.

Then on a retreat at Mt. St. Frances in Southern Indiana, I received a full healing in the form of a vision and a story of how God saw the event. I saw what Jesus saw and what He did.

At the retreat while praying alone, suddenly I was not there anymore. . .

I looked from my right to my left and all around me. I was in the room where I was raped. I was watching from the other side of the room. I could see me crying and struggling beneath the perpetrator. I felt the violence of his actions against my body. Then I saw my body give out and go slack. One of my arms fell along side of the bed.

It was then that I saw Jesus on the floor by the side of the bed. He was on bended knee His head bowed in sorrow and pain. He was there with me. Jesus was experiencing my pain. Then he reached up and took my hand in His and said,

"He may get your body, but he will not get your soul."

BENJAMIN

At 26, I became pregnant for a third time. This time it was a set of twins! I thought, "Oh boy! I sure hope God lets me keep at least one of them!" I was right. He let me keep one of them.

I had to spend my first five months in bed due to severe morning sickness and in the third month, one of the babies passed. By my sixth month I had settled down into the routine of working and being pregnant.

One day, I was sitting at my desk, doing my book- keeping work, when I heard a child's voice along side of me say, " Mommy, I am a little boy." I knew this was my baby's spirit talking to me. I giggled and said, "How do you know you are a little boy?" Benjamin replied, "God told me."

All the voices I tell you I clearly hear are audible, outside of my body, not in my mind. It is as if someone is standing right next to me.

I believe this is why in the Catholic prayer, one line reads as follows:

> *I believe in God, the Father Almighty,*
> *Creator of Heaven and Earth.*
> *Of all that is seen and unseen.*

Amen and amen.

A DAY AT THE FAIR

When I was still married to Clarence and we were living in Lanesville, for awhile, he was taking seizure medication to help with his anger. He was quite pleasant natured. One Sunday afternoon there was a psychic fair going on over in Louisville. Clarence thought it might be fun to go over and people watch.

We loaded up the kids, then, age seven, four and a half, and three years old. We took off for downtown. When we got to the hotel there were lots of people mulling around. The children were very good as we went from vendor to vendor.

One person was set up to test people's abilities. Law of averages stated out of 15 cards you could get three right. Clarence and David got five right each. Ben and I got six each. The lady explained that there were some gifts there and we should be aware of our instincts.

Since Andy was only three we thought we were through and went to leave. He spoke up and said, "I want to play too! I want to play too!" He thought we were playing a game, and he was being left out! She got the cards back out and showed him the shapes; stars, squares, circles and crosses. She turned them over and shuffled them and started.

"Tell me what you see in your mind, Andy," she said to him. Right away and fast he started saying shapes. I said, "Slow down, son. Don't say the same one every time." The psychic told me to "Shut up!"

She hollered, "Keep going Andy!" She was very excited! When he was finished, he got eight out of 15 right, and he was three years old! That was unheard of!

She was shaking and hollering. "He has a gift! A strong gift! You have to help him develop this! He has to be trained!"

98

By that time we were smiling and walking backwards towards the door. We thanked her for her time and turned to get out of Dodge! We left quickly. We did not know what to do with this new revelation about our littlest boy.

God gives every good soul gifts of the Spirit. Whether you use them for the benefit of His Kingdom or this world, is up to you.
Who do you serve with your gifts?

PEACE

By the time I was 32 years old, I had three little boys, a home in the country, and I was still married to Clarence, my first husband.

For awhile I had been feeling poorly. I went to see my physician. He examined me and then started explaining what he had found. He was telling me he had found an eight to ten millimeter mass wrapped around my colon.

I did not have enough understanding to be alarmed about what it could be.

All of a sudden I heard a voice. It said, *"Be not alarmed. All is not as it appears."* Great peace came over me, and I was never afraid. I was very sick, but not afraid. Three doctors declined to do my surgery.

The prayer group at our local Catholic church, St. Mary's, came by and prayed over me. They all laid hands on me, and I felt something so strong I cried and cried. Clarence stood and watched. He would not participate.

I eventually had surgery. All it was, was my fallopian tube had become infected and enlarged. It had wrapped around my colon. It ended up being a half hour surgery, and I went home a few days later.

NO SCHOOL!

Several of the years Clarence and I lived in Lanesville, were big snow years. He worked third shift at a cigarette factory. We had one child in second grade, one in kindergarten and one still at home. We usually watched local channel three for the weather.

On this one particular night there was no bad weather approaching us. School was open as usual. Well, for some reason I could not get four year old Andy to settle down to bed that night. He was jumping on his bed and laughing! I said in my best mommy voice , "Son! You are keeping your brothers up! It is late and they have school tomorrow!" While still jumping on the bed he responded, " No Mommy, it is going to snow tonight. There will be no school! We can stay up!"

I argued the weathermen on the television had said nothing about snow coming to us. It was all to no avail. I finally got him to settle down after 11 pm and go to sleep. What a night!

The next morning we woke up to 14 inches of snow. A fluke they called it on the TV. No school for Southern Indiana. We called it "eerie" and started listening to the four year old when he talked.

** This is the same kid as he was growing up we could never beat him in the game Clue. When it came to his turn, he just said what it was. He always knew.

In the new version that we all played recently in 2010, Andy was with us, and his character was killed off before he got to play his turn. This ended up being the first game we ever got to play to the finish!

HEILIGE NACHT
HOLY NIGHT

In 1996, I was 37 years old and newly divorced from Clarence. I met a man who lived up near Ohio. Sometimes I would go up to see him on a weekend. I usually took $35.00 with me for the trip for gas and what ever I might need on the road. He would go on Saturday mornings to work to cash his paycheck. It was during that time I would go for a walk. I got up that particular Saturday morning, and got ready to go on my walk when I heard an audible voice say, "Take money." I felt in my spirit it was the Lord, but I said, "Lord, I'm only going for a walk. I don't need any money." I heard a little stronger, " Take money." Because I am insolent, I said again, "Lord, I am not going anywhere I will need money for!" I walked out the door.

I got to the spot where I usually turned around to go back and I again hear an audible voice, "Turn here." "But Lord," I cried, "I don't want to go that way! I turn to go back home here!" I heard very firmly, "**Turn here!!**"

I sighed. "Evidently there is something you want me to do so you just take control of this vessel, my feet and guide me where you want me to go." And off I went!

Down the street there was a block yard sale going on. I passed yard sale after yard sale until I finally got to an estate sale with antiques. Walking past everyone all the way to the backyard to the very back of the lot, before me stood an old bread rack. I bent down to the bottom rung and pulled out an almost 200 year old engraving print of *"The Birth of Christ in Bethlehem."* It had a price of $100.00 on it. It had been left on the baker's rack by mistake.

I went back up to the front, picture in hand. I asked to speak to the person in charge. It ended up being four brothers. I told the oldest, "Gather up your brothers, I have a story to tell you." I told them the whole story, and how I only had $35.00. Then I told them I would stand over by the side and they could discuss what they wanted to do. They all looked at each other and the oldest said, "Miss, I don't think it's up to us. Go home and get your $35.00. Sold to you."

I went back and got my money and my car and brought the picture home.

The relationship ended six months later.

I still have the picture beautifully framed by my wonderful husband Mark, as a Christmas present to our new home on Mathes Road in 2003. We took the picture with us when we sold our home. It awaits it's final home.

So do we.

WALKING WITH JESUS

In early 1996 I had a dream I was walking with Jesus in the Sinai Desert. I could feel the warm sand beneath my feet and hot dry air all around me.

I was crying. I told Him how I had loved Him all my life. The circumstances of an abusive marriage and now being alone seemed so unfair. Couldn't He please send me a good husband to help me and my sons?

Jesus listened to all my cares and concerns. Then He held up His hand. He said simply, "I will send you someone to walk your path with you."

That was the year Mark Peyron became born again in the Holy Spirit. He sang in tongues for over 45 minutes. That was when he turned his heart to God.

We met in November of 1997.

In 1996 Mark went to a family reunion. Their picture was in the local paper. They named Mark with his wife, Debbie. At the time no one was with him and he had no girlfriend much less a wife.

The year before he met me he dreamed of going bowling with a family he had never seen before. It was me and the boys.

We married on August 7, 1999.

I could argue against pre-destiny, but I think I know too much. Or just maybe, it's choices. Choices set before us. Like when Jesus said, "Choose life and have it to the full."

What a wonderful idea.

What if everybody chose life to the full?

WAIT FOR IT!

After my divorce from Clarence, the boys and I still managed to do nice things. We went on a few trips, vacations, day excursions to the local amusement park in the summer and fall, picnics and family nights. We made joyful times to help us all heal. When my boys were growing up, the amusement park in the summer was their favorite place to go! I'd make sandwiches and drinks, and off we'd go, over the river to the city for a day of fun in the sun at the pool, park and rides.

We'd usually start pool side where it wasn't so crowded. The boys would race around the Lazy River. I would paddle and take my time, relaxing. There was a strong undercurrent that kept the water flowing around the river. When you got to the area where you get out, the current was strong enough to knock a person over if you were not careful.

While I was still going around the river with the boys being way ahead of me racing each other, I saw a lovely picture playing out in front of me. A Momma was on her raft with a little boy, maybe 18 months old, in her lap. He had the look of a Downs Syndrome baby. He was trying to lap up the water. Momma was ever so gently stopping him every time. It was an adorable picture. At the time I wondered at this significance but gave God thanks for it anyway.

When it came this lady's turn for getting out of the pool, she was ahead of me. I had just gotten to the area as she was stepping out. The water was maybe two and a half feet where she was and over four feet out where I was.

All of a sudden in my spirit, out loud like someone was standing next to me, I heard, *"Stop, wait for it!"*

Then I saw as in slow motion, the baby slip from his mother's arms down into the water, being sucked down into the undercurrent, out to the river area. I heard again, out loud, *"Wait for it!"* I saw the baby going deeper and deeper under the water, heading straight for me. The frantic mother was fighting, trying to get through the crowd. Then I heard *"Now! Now!"* I dove down into the water, grabbed the baby and came up.

He blew out bubbles, sputtered and squirmed in my arms. He was okay! The mother came running in the water as fast as she could towards us. I popped that baby on my other hip with a strong grip on him, held out my hand and said, "Calm down!" She was visibly crying, "I'm not mad at him! I couldn't get all those x'!*# people to move!" I handed her baby back to her and he immediately tried to wiggle out of her arms. She exited the pool quickly, baby in her arms, and said not one word of thanks to me. It's okay. The safe baby was thanks enough for me.

HOLY

In the fall of 1996, I was attending a local state college in Southern Indiana. I thought I was going into Medical Assisting. One of our classes was on a Friday morning. The teacher was a very nice, middle aged man. He was a fireman, a coroner and he was never on time for class! It was a long class, two and a half hours. I guess he figured he could teach advanced first aid in one hour forty-five minutes flat each week. (*What-ever*)

The students would arrive on time and wait for him. Some people would bring their breakfast and eat, others would sit in a click and talk about what they were planning for the weekend. I would usually sit and read my bible. I was in the second chair in the second to last row. There were very nice ladies all around me.

On one Friday morning while I was reading and the rest were waiting for the teacher, one of the girls in the next row over started calling my name. It took me a few seconds to realize she was calling me because I didn't know anyone knew my name! The girls on each side of me and one behind me were waiting for my attention.

I looked up and saw they wanted to talk with me. I closed my bible and asked what I could help them with. One of the girls wanted my opinion on some things that had been happening to her. I told her I would be happy to hear her stories.

She was a tall, blond, big framed girl and very pleasant to talk to with a ready laugh. Her family unit consisted of three children and her mother. Her husband had left her.

One spring they were planning a vacation to the beach. Everyone was looking forward to it. While on vacation she started having very vivid dreams of her youngest son dying in a car crash. The feelings came on her so strong that on the last day of their vacation, she decided to keep them out on the beach, to "wear their little butts out" playing and then drive home. That way, they'd be sound asleep and wouldn't feel a thing when the accident would happen.

Off they went to head back home. They got up towards the top of Florida when she saw, on the other side of the expressway, a van veer off the road and go down the embankment into a ditch. She immediately pulled her van over and ran through all four lanes of traffic plus the median. Her mother actually thought she was hit by an oncoming truck because there was no way he could have missed her. She did not remember crossing the road at all. She only remembered being at the side of the van and working on getting everyone out safely.

There was a mother, a father, and several children. The van had over turned with the back end dug deep into the sand. Gas and oil were spewing and sizzling on the engine. She knew she had to work fast to get everyone out alive.

The mother and the father were the first ones helped out and up to the side of the road. Then she went back for two children. When she got up to the embankment with them, the parents got frantic. Where's the youngest? Where's their third child? Where's their little boy?

Back down into the vehicle she went. She started calling his name out. No answer. That was when she started digging into the sand looking for him. She found his body with his head completely buried in the sand. Digging harder and faster, she finally pulled him out of the sand and out of the van. She laid him on the ground. His face, nose and mouth were all caked in sand. He was not breathing. She dug sand out of his mouth and nose and eyes. She then discovered this six year old boy

108

was a twin to her six year old son. This was the boy in her dream! She started CPR until the paramedics got there and took over.

By God's grace and an obedient daughter, the little boy lived. Despite the fact that he had been without oxygen for almost half an hour, there was no permanent brain damage either. Now that's God!

Her next story was just as amazing! She had gone to bed one evening when she dreamed of running across a large field. She was out in the country running very fast! She got to a roadway and saw a car in a ditch. She ran down to the car and opened the door. There sitting, bloodied and hurt, was her pastor's 17 year old son. She helped him up to the side of the road. Then she took off running through the same field. She woke up the next morning feeling very exhausted.

A few days later at her church, her pastor got up and thanked everyone for their prayers for his 17 year old son that had been in an automobile accident. He also related the story the young man told the ambulance drivers when they got to him. They could not see how with his injuries he had gotten safely up to the street. He told them one of his dad's church members showed up in her pajamas to help him. He guessed she must have lived nearby and heard the car go off the road.

No, she did not live close by.

These are instances of what are called bi-location which is to appear in two places at once. The body is in one and the spirit in another. I gently tell her she is a very special child of God to be able to do these things. She said she is not worthy, she drinks, she parties, and she is a single mom. I told her maybe God sees her differently than she sees herself. He sees her as special. Maybe she should start seeing herself the way God sees her.

Then she related this last story.

She had a favorite aunt that was dying in the hospital. She picked up her mother and they went to be by her bedside along with some other family members.

She didn't remember anything after walking through the doors into the room. Her mother related the occurrences after she came to.

She walked into the room and sat next to her aunt saying over and over, "Wait for it, wait for it, wait for it," Then suddenly she yelled, " Her mother and father are here for her and she is leaving!" At that point her aunt breathed her last. It wasn't until after everyone had left the room that she came to again.

I told her because of the amazing things she sees God has great plans for her. Then I asked her why she spoke to me of these things instead of her pastor.

She replied simply, "Because you are holy."

FIRST ANNIVERSARY

When the boys were little, I dated a local gentleman who owned a car mechanics shop. The brakes on my car were giving out, so he traded me cars for the day while he fixed them. To thank him, I made him dinner for the five of us. He stayed and joined us for family night. This consisted of movies, popcorn and snacks.

By the end of the evening, Andy and David had fallen asleep on the couches and we were sitting on the floor. Ben had already gone to bed. I picked up David and Marshall picked up Andy. We put them in their beds. They both slept in the same bedroom across from each other. I tucked David in and kissed him goodnight. Then I turned around to tuck Andy in and kiss him goodnight. He was sitting straight up in bed. Marshall was at the end of Andy's bed. I said to Andy, "What are you doing awake son?" Andy replied sleepily, " I want to play with Nate." I giggled. "Honey, we don't know anyone named Nate." Andy insisted, "Nate is here and he wants to play." About this time Marshall left the room.

Congenially, I told Andy, "Okay, you lay down to bed. I kiss you good night. Nate lay down to bed. I kiss Nate good night. Good night Andy. Good night Nate." I kissed Andy as he curled up under the covers and went to sleep.

I found Marshall sitting on the edge of my bed with his head in his hands. I started the conversation giggling again, "You won't believe this, Andy doesn't even know a Nate, but he sure wanted to play with him." At that, Marshall looked up at me crying big crocodile tears. Alarmed I cried out, "What's wrong?"

He said, " Yes, he does know a Nate. Nate is my son, and he died one year ago today. This is the first anniversary of his death."

To the best of my understanding, Andy is able to see attached spirits.   He was four years old at the time.

APPARITION

A couple of years after the divorce of my first husband, the boys were spending a few weeks over the summer with him. He lived in a little white house along Big Indian Creek. Andy, our youngest, was six years old at the time.

One afternoon he was playing in the open shed in the side yard. He saw a man, very pale, and all dressed in white, walking through the yard. He went to the creek's edge. Andy went up to talk to him, and he disappeared.

When I got the boys back for the rest of the summer, Andy told me of this occurrence. I explained as best I could. Possibly a man had drowned maybe many years ago in the creek at that site. He must be compelled occasionally to revisit the area. Most people can't see such things when they happen.

I told him he was a special child to see such things. He still is.

WARNING!

When Mark and I were first married, maybe not quite two years, all the boys were living with us. We were a lively household. I worked part time so I could be home when the kids got off the bus after school.

One day I came in shortly after the guys got home. Ben had given a ride to someone he met at the local coffee shop. I came through the living room and saw this man in the kitchen. Up until then, anyone our children had brought over as friends we treated as family. Hello! How are ya! Nice to meet you. Are you hungry?

Not this time. This boy looked at me, and I stopped. He was dark, and I don't mean his color. There was black all around him. I said to my son, "Ben, honey, can I see you in the back bedroom?' He said, "Sure Momma."

I stayed very calm.

"Son, you have to get this man out of our house. Lose him. Make sure he can never find his way back here again. I've never told you that you can't have a friend, but not this one, son." He nodded his head yes, walked into the kitchen and said, "Come on, we have to leave."

About five years later, this man went on a killing spree. He killed several family members while robbing them. He is in prison for life.

When God sends you messages, inclinations, warnings, heed them.

It may well save your life.

"911"

Do you remember when I wrote previously in this book several times, that when warnings come it is not necessarily to stop what is going to happen but to prepare you?

These are some of those times. I had no understanding on the first one until six months after the events.

In August of 2001, I dreamed twice of flying on a jet plane. Both times my sister, Vicki was on the plane with me besides all the other passengers. That was how I knew it was a dream because you would never get my sister to fly anywhere on any plane!

In the first dream we were in the plane, and it was having trouble staying aloft. Everyone was scared. It was a very quick dream.

The next week I had a more detailed dream. We were on the same plane. We were flying along a river I did not know. I'm from a river city, along the mighty Ohio. It was not that river. I looked up and saw a very tall building. I knew in my heart we weren't going to clear it. We were flying too low. I started screaming, **"Pull up! Pull up! You are going to hit the building!"** When I had looked out the window in the airplane, and I saw the river, it looked like an animation, of a map maybe. When I woke up I thought it was so odd to be dreaming this. I was not planning to fly anywhere. Six months after 9/11, I saw on the news, a reproduction of what happened and what the passengers saw out their windows. They did this in animation. It was the exact same view I had seen in my dream.

114

Several years later, I had another dream that there was going to be another attack on a major bank building in America. I could see a big block type van, white, going under a viaduct heading straight for a large urban building. This time I started praying for God's help! The next week I saw on the television newscast, where the FBI and the CIA had stopped a plan from foreign terrorists to car bomb one of our major cities banking complexes. They showed what the rout looked like and the type of vehicle that was going to be used. It was all the same as in my dream.

At this point I am listening very closely to all telling or warning dreams.

THE WAY

In 1998, Mark and I were at Holy Thursday Mass at St. Michael's. We were engaged at the time. The boys were spending Easter week with Clarence. After mass, Mark came back to my apartment and stayed with me. I got up at 4 am to eat a snack. I was hungry. A poem started appearing in my head.

The first line went through, I thought, "Gee, that was interesting." The second line went through my head and I stopped eating. In the middle of the third line, I was grabbing second grade paper and a broken pencil. I started writing as hard and as fast as I could. At one point I couldn't keep up so I cried out, "Please! I lost that last line! Please back up and give it to me again!" It did.

When I finished all 32 lines, I went upstairs and woke Mark. I read to him the Easter Story the Lord had given me. What a blessing!

You see, I am not a poet the way I am not a writer, until God comes in the picture. Then, I am everything He called me to be.

What about you?

THE   WAY

It was the night before Easter and all through the house,
Not a creature was stirring, not even a mouse.
The prisoners were hung on their trees as onlookers cried,
In hopes that our Lord would come down, if only He tried.
There we stood at His feet, so despondent, so despaired,
As our Lord bowed His head, the ground shook,
The veil in the temple teared.
We took Him down and buried Him in a fresh hewn cave,
That Joseph of Arimethea thought he might save.
And on the third day there arose such a clatter,
We arose from our room to see what was the matter.
It was the women of our group, shouting in the street,
"Come in", we cried, "so we can all meet."
Magdalene said with tears in her eyes,
"He said He would. He said He would rise!"
I said, "Hold on, wait a minute. Tell this story true.
What on this earth has happened to you?"
"We went to His tomb to anoint Him with oil.
We worried on how we'd move the rock,
on this we did toil.
But when we got there, the rock was all cleared.
We thought this was strange when a young man appeared.
He said to us, "Why dost thou look for the living among
the dead?
Look there, up the road ahead."
A man was walking, to him I did cry,
"Sir, did you see any passers by?"
And He said, "Mary, it is I."
After His forty days so did He ascend,
To His Glory, His Kingdom, till the Earth comes to an end.
What is the meaning of this story do you say?
That Jesus lived and died for us to show us The Way.

Jesus said unto her, "I am the resurrection, and the life: he that believth in me, though he were dead, yet shall he live: And whosoever liveth and believeth in me shall never die. Believeth thou this?
John 11:25-26

<u>Believeth thou this?</u>

MEMORIUM

The summer after the healing of my back. I was working in my dining room on patient assistance work. The date was July 5th. Our oldest son Ben was in the army in basic training. He had called me earlier that week complaining about chest pain. I told him to take his heart rate and tell his CO. I asked him to call me back when he could.

Early that morning of the 5th, I received a clairaudient warning. This is what I heard. Out loud.

Memorium

> *And I will meet you in the garden,*
> *where life all begins anew,*
> *roses, flowers, jasmine,*
> *there I will wait for you.*

Immediately I knew Ben was dying. I fell on the floor and pleaded with God. "Lord, I know you sent your son to save me. I am begging you not to take my son away from me. Not my son. Take another."

Just about that time our neighbor Melanie knocked on the door. I was crying. She asked me what was wrong! I told her I knew Ben was dying. She cried with me. One hour later Andy our youngest son came running into the house yelling, "Momma! Momma! Something's wrong with Ben!" I cried back, "I know! I know! I'm waiting for a call now!"

Andy and I sat in the kitchen area by the phone and waited for the call. It came one hour later. Ben was indeed in the hospital and had a possible heart attack. They were going to have to medically discharge him. His blood pressure was 210/140 and his heart rate was above 200!

119

He should've stroked, but he didn't. I believe because of our warnings and prayers to God, Ben was spared.

We went to see him three weeks later in Oklahoma. Another young man in another platoon, the week after Ben's episode, died of the same heart condition.

Benjamin is still with us to this day.

DANIEL

In the fall of 2001, my father-in-law, Daniel Louis Peyron, age 76, went home to be with the Lord two weeks before we were taking the vacation of a lifetime! The boys were very brave. They told Mark they understood if we had to cancel everything and go the next year. After much prayer, Mark decided that Grandpa would want us to go ahead and go. Full steam ahead!

We picked up the conversion van we were renting for the trip. It was all set up and vacation ready. It had a television, a VCR and ear phones for each child! Yay! Off we went to Walt Disney World in Florida. We had been saving all year long.

We got there and everything was wonderful! I had called after it was decided to still go and talked to one of the managers. I asked her to please send a card or a little spray of flowers or something to show condolences. Boy, did they.

They upgraded our room at the Contemporary from a garden view to the 10th story and a view of the Cinderella's Castle at night! They sent two dozen roses and two cards and gifts as condolences. This is one example of why we still vacation at Walt Disney World.

We had been there several days, and one evening when the boys were out together in the hotel, we were back in our room having a little quiet time by ourselves.

I looked over at the wall across from us, and I saw a large man's shadow. In my eyes, it looked like he turned to us and smiled! I could see this apparition smiling! So I smiled back and said, "Mark, I think your dad is here with us. I can see him. He is smiling and he is very happy for you." Before Mark could say anything, the boys came through the door. Andy said, "Grandpa just walked down the hall with us!" Absolutely he did!

121

WANTED

I have a friend named Lisa. She is a very busy mom of four small children and step mother to two teenage girls. Back, before she was so busy, in the spring of 2002, she had a very interesting occurrence happen.

Lisa is a lovely young lady. She exudes joyful kindness. Many times, that comes in handy! Lisa and her husband, Jim were new to the Southern Indiana area. Wanting to help her new husband and to please God, she started praying about getting a job. She went to the phone book and began to pray. Then she opened the yellow pages and called the first place she saw.

Well, at the same time she was doing this, at the place she was calling, the lady in charge was sitting and praying about hiring another person and who to hire.

Lisa went right over and talked to her and got the job that very day!

After all, when two people are in agreement on one subject before the Lord, His answer is yes and Amen! Glory to God!

GENEVA

I have belonged to a Charismatic prayer group for over twenty years. They meet at a little Catholic Church in Southern Indiana on Thursday evenings at 7 pm. These fine, decent people supported me through a difficult divorce, and celebrated with me for my happy marriage now. In my 20 years there, and my husband Mark's 12 years there, we have seen some mighty interesting things. Even mystical.

In 2003, we were at prayer group one Thursday evening with our regular group in attendance. Phil and Melanie were there, our leaders and main musicians, they started the group 25 years ago after their born again experience. Melanie's little sister was there too, Mary, also on guitar and back up vocalist. Mark, Barbara, Wayne, Miss Geneva, and a few others of us were there.

Mark and I were still very Catholic in those days. We were learning more about how to walk in the gifts of the charisms as we understood them. Miss Geneva, the oldest of our group, was telling a story. It was about the time she saw the Holy Spirit come down over the priest during the mass at communion time. She saw the misty grey cloud descend from the ceiling and rest over the priest. While she related this story, I started seeing all around her head, neck and hands, a green glow. It was very prominent.

In my natural mind I thought my blood pressure must be up and started taking my pulse. Until my husband Mark, who was sitting next to me, leaned over to me and said, " Do you see that green glow around Geneva's head, neck and arms?" Well, dears, I got all excited, he got all excited, we told what just happened, and then everybody got excited! We knew it was a manifestation of some kind from the Holy Spirit but not sure what.

Eventually, a pastor friend of mine, Ivie, told us what the color from around Geneva meant. Green was for healing and harvest time. And what Geneva saw was the Shekinah Glory of God! The Glory cloud! What Moses saw in the desert.

Geneva had gifts of sight. Mark had gifts of sight. I had gifts of sight. Before this time, we did not recognize that we had such gifts. But it makes sense. Listen.

Coincidence? I think not. One visionary just happens to meet and marry another visionary? No. I think our spirits recognized each other. They were in harmony. The bible calls it "well yoked." Our bodies and personalities were just along for the ride.

What are your gifts and who are you sharing them with?

TORNADO!

The end of May 2003 brought dangerous weather across the west and mid-west, driving east across the continental United States. The weekend of Memorial Day was the most weather violent since the great outbreak of tornadoes in 1973.

That Friday night, some friends of ours had their roof dislodged from their home. They came to stay with us on Saturday. That night was only a precursor of what was to come on Sunday.

Sunday was the graduation of our niece, Sarah from high school. Since the school was only a block from my mother-in-law's home, the family parked there and walked over to the school.

As we were walking, suddenly between my eyes, I got a severe stabbing pain. I said to Mark, "Something's wrong with the weather." My husband replied, "No honey, the weatherman said the next bad front won't be here until tonight."

Out of my spirit, not checking in with my brain or my mouth, I said, " You are believing a lie." He said, "What did you say?" The second time I said it, I heard it with my ears. I said, " You are believing a lie." There was no more conversation.

We went inside and found seats with the rest of the family. The graduation soon began. The graduating class proceeded in and the speeches started. We were sitting along the side wall where people came into the building. I heard the door open and saw three police officers hurry to the dignitaries seated on the stage. One of the dignitaries got up and came to the podium.

"There has just been a tornado warning issued for Clark County. We must have an orderly procession into the hallway," he stated calmly.

Our area was the first one out towards the back of the building. We all went into the hallways and waited. "I am so scared, I don't want to die!" I cried to Mark. He just looked at me sadly. Then a young lady came running down the hallway for all she's worth yelling, " Get down! Get down! It's headed right for us!"

Crying and with knees trembling instead of hunkering down, I got up and went to the middle of the hallway. I told my husband as I got up, " I am not going out of this world this way. I'm praying to God!"

I started hollering at the top of my lungs! "Father God in Heaven! Jesus who calmed the stormy seas! In your names I baptize every person in this building in the name of the Father, Son and Holy Spirit. Every single soul is yours Heavenly Father! We are your children! You have counted the hairs on our heads! I ask you now, Father, in the name of Jesus, to send the tornado back to hell from where it came! Tornado, you will not hurt one single person here! We are God's children. You will leave and not touch one single brick of this building nor the area around it. You go back to hell where you are from!" A group of African American women started singing hymns and church songs while I prayed.

Within seconds, a girl came running through again this time saying, "It passed over us! It passed over us!" I went back to sit with my husband, my knees still shaking. It was not a few minutes later when the same girl came back down the hall, running and yelling again, 'Get down! Get down! Another one is headed right for us!"

This time heads turned toward me in a snap! The ladies started singing. That was my cue. I got up again a little more boldly this time. I rebuked the wind in Jesus' name. I called it back into hell a second time. Glory to God! And a second time that day, the tornado popped

126

back up in the sky and went over us. In a few minutes we got the all clear sign.

By that time, my nerves had had it. I headed for the bathroom. All the way there, I was thanking God for hearing my call and saving us. I went into the bathroom praising God loudly, when I realized there were feet in the stall next to me. Sheepishly, I said to her, "Sorry. I didn't know anyone else was in here. You probably think I am a religious nut." She said to me, "I think you are the most spirit filled person I've ever seen." I thanked her, and she told me to continue praying because we could all use it. I did so.

We were almost back in the gym when we saw the local weatherman on the television in the main hall. We stopped to listen. He was standing there by himself in the studio. He said, " Ladies and gentlemen, the tornado is heading straight for our station. I sent everyone to safety. I will stay here on the air with you until the end. Pray for me."

I got on my knees with tears in my eyes and started praying once again, "Lord God, save your child! He has called out for prayer! We again ask for Your divine intervention! Save him!" A third time, the tornado went back up in the air and over the studio.

When it was safe to leave the building, we ran back to my mother-in-law's home. I told my husband we couldn't stay long. We had to get back home. More are coming. I could feel it. We had to help our neighbors! This time Mark did not disagree. We went home a little later that afternoon. All our area was safe. The weather had gone north of us in Corydon.

By dinnertime, the sky looked ominous once again. We turned on the television and saw tornadic activity two counties away from us. We started making phone calls. We called our children home. We called friends who had no basements. We called a pastor and her family and her dogs. We called friends who lived in a trailer, and we called our neighbors who lived around us. By the evening, we had eleven people and two dogs in our basement.

Pastor Ivie and I went along our home and property edges earlier that evening with anointed oil. We had prayed a hedge of protection over our land and everyone in it. We soon lost electricity. We brought all our candles downstairs. We brought our hurricane lamps. We also brought food and drinks, water, and the battery operated short band weather radio too. Within a few minutes people were drinking, munching, and playing cards and games. They laughed and said, "Only the Peyron's could turn a tornado into a party!"

All of a sudden you could not see outside. Outside it was coal black. White rain covered the area. Winds were whipping all around our home. We prayed God shore us up one more time that day. Our am radio station 84 WHAS was stating Corydon took a direct hit! Everyone stayed the night either upstairs or downstairs on beds, pullouts, or couches with blankets and candles.

The next morning Mark and I were up on the back deck making coffee the old fashioned way, pancakes on a griddle and orange juice for all our guests! We still had hot water, thanks to having two 40 gallon hot water tanks.

Looking off the back of our deck, four trees past our one and a half acres, the tornado had come through. It looked like a giant had stepped on the trees in the neighbors acres and laid them over flat. The barn roof was peeled back. The horses had been let out into the back field and would not go back into their stalls. The tornado had picked up their single wide with people in it and set it right back down on the ground.

The 170 mph winds had come down in the creek

128

one mile from us and went right past our land. The only damage we had was a bent flag pole and a broken window screen. Mark fixed the flagpole right back in place, and the screen was still sitting right below the window so we popped it right back in place too!

The roads had debris all over them and it was awhile before people could get out and travel on them to get back to their homes.

Wow. God is good. Every prayer was answered.

MEETING YESHI

In the year 2003, one morning, on first waking up and getting out of bed, I heard a voice from outside my head as if standing next to me, say to me, "Call me Yeshi, thanks." I knew it was the Son of God. I smiled and said, "Nice to meet you." I felt in my heart this was a term used for him when he was young.

VERIFICATION

In November of 2007, my husband and I met a wonderful man named Carl Andrews while on vacation at Walt Disney World. He was a Messianic Jew. For several years we corresponded. For my 50th birthday, Carl sent me a Complete Jewish Bible. I read it cover to cover. On page 1600, in the back of the book in the glossary, under Yeshua (Jesus)- it stated the ancient pronunciation in the Galil, where Yeshua grew up, he would have been called Yeshu.

When I heard Him in 2003, I was not given the spelling. Being off by one letter in my southern Kentucky dialect and hearing, is not an impossibility.

He introduced himself with the name his mother would have called him on this earth when he was a little boy.

Yeshi is my best friend.

GOING HOME

I have a friend named Joan. She has spent most of her life working for the Lord. Her health has not always been the best, and right now her health is quite poor. One day, when we brought food over for she and her family, and to visit, she shared with me many stories that have no natural explanations. But they sure make a good read!

Several years back, she had a good friend named Jim. He and his wife had a precious little five year old daughter. Much to their dismay, the little girl was diagnosed with Leukemia. This was not a particularly religious family, making no mention of Jesus in the house. At least not yet!

One night, while the little girl was very ill, sitting in her bedroom, the parents heard her talking to someone. They went into the room and asked who she was talking to. She said it was a man named Jesus.

Imagine their astonishment!

They asked what he had to say. She replied, " He says I am going to live with him and not to be afraid."

She died shortly after that.

What a witness to her family! What a reassurance!
"To be absent from the body is to be present with the Lord."

WALNUTS

Joan had friends named Joyce and Jim. Jim became very ill. Subsequently, they told Joan about it. Jim had a brain tumor. They asked Joan to pray over him. She complied. Joan prayed a very simple prayer, that the brain tumor would dry up and die. It would look like a dead walnut.

Well, each day Jim felt a little better and a little better. He went back to his doctor on his scheduled visit, and they took an x-ray.

The doctor came out and said, "This cancer has dried up like a walnut!"

The cancer died and Jim didn't.

That's what happens when believer's tell the problem specifically what to do in Jesus' name, and it did. In short order!

Just like Jesus did when he cursed the fig tree for having no fruit.

God likes everything and everyone to be fruitful. Fruit on a tree or in a person. We should always be about planting seeds where ever they will grow!

After all, God loves orchards. They were all over the Garden of Eden!

JOAN AND THE DEMONS!

If you think sickness is natural and not demonic, you better read this!!

Back in 1990 at Christmastime, Joan had pneumonia. It started in November and kept lingering.

She was so cold one evening, and she was going downhill fast! The next thing she saw in the door way was herself! She was having an out of the body experience! She saw her own body still in the bed!

There were little demons all around her. They were going very fast all around the ceiling and the bed. They were very ugly to look at and were intent on agonizing her. Horrible sounds emitted from their throats. They motioned for her to come with them!

Then she saw two lights shimmering around her, one was about 12 inches from her and the other 18 or so inches away. They looked like globes that came down through the ceiling. She felt heat radiating off of them.

Her spirit went back into her body. Her pastor came over that night and she told him what she had seen. He told her she had battled satan!

By the next morning she was still so ill, the family put her in the hospital. This is man's way of helping but God has a better way!

While in the hospital, the demons came back! These were even smaller than the first ones. Joan again left her body. She looked at the walls of her room. There were lights, colors and pictures of two friends who had died. Then God Himself showed up and said to her, *"NOW LET ME SHOW YOU SOME OF MY GLORY!"* She could hear Christmas music. She became warm again and her health turned around. She had God's promise on it! Wow, what a doctor! The King of doctors!

The King of the Universe!

FRED

Our Pastor has been born again and called to preach for over 33 years as of the year 2010. He is a professional musician, playing along side him is his wife, Jeanne and his best friend, Bill Mauck.

Shortly after he was born again in the winter of 1977, he got to meet Jesus.

One evening Fred was in his kitchen in a little town in Illinois. He turned around and there stood Jesus in his kitchen. He saw Jesus in the flesh, very real and tangible.

Then Jesus spoke to Fred, "Let go." Fred replied, "I can't. I'm afraid. What if I get hurt?" Jesus explained to him, "I have put angels in front of you lest you dash your foot upon the ground. Let go, Fred. Let go."

Fred thought for a moment and then he said, "Alright. I will. I'll let go." Jesus then told him he was having a heart attack but he would be okay now. He would stay here for now.

At the last word from Jesus' mouth, angels led Fred down as he fell from the sky. He went into what he thought was a cool, dry valley. That is when he fell into his own mouth, into his own body. His body felt very heavy. He wanted to stay out and go with Jesus, but it was not his time.

Because Jesus conquered death, Pastor Fred has beaten death many times in his life. And God is no respecter of persons, what He does for one, He will do for another. Even you.

NEAR DEATH EXPERIENCE

In the spring of 2008, I met a lady who was an LPN, at a new job I had taken. We sat together in class. She told me this story about her husband.

He is a Lakota Indian. They are both spirit filled Christians. At this time he was very ill. The year before he had died right in front of her. He was clinically dead for 40 minutes. This is his near death experience.

While his body was dead, his spirit rose up and went to the ceiling. He could see people running around to try to save him. He could see his wife in the bathroom crying. They had been married 33 years.

Then he went to a higher place. It was all white. He could see his glorified body. He saw Jesus Christ. He knew Him. The elders of his tribe were there also. They took him before God.

His wife relates that he still cries when he tells this story. He felt filled with the Holy Spirit. God's love came over him and infiltrated his whole being. It was a stronger feeling than there are words to tell. He then came back in order to tell his story and give hope to people.

Here is his story and there is your hope in Jesus' resurrection.

THE MOUNTAIN OF THE LORD

It was a Sunday evening and we were at the 6 pm service at Believer's Fellowship. Mark and I were sitting in the chairs in the back row.

Our pastor, Fred Schuppert, was teaching on Exodus 19, The Mountain of the Lord. He started out with "I am bringing you into myself" quote from scripture. This hit home for me because of the dream I had recently about God telling me He is bringing me back to Himself in the fall of my 54th year. I thought it meant my time was up here in the fall of 2012, but it ends up there may be another way you can interpret this!

Fred said we are a peculiar treasure. I was thinking, "Yep, that's me. Peculiar all my life." We are predestine, a kingdom of priests, people set apart for His service. When. Now! We who are born again are called out of the darkness! We are drawn into the living light of the bible! Psalm 4:3-5 *"The Lord hath set apart him that is godly for himself. The Lord will hear when I call unto Him."* When he got to verse five it started glowing in yellow! Right before my eyes! My confirmation? Again, my husband for the second time in our lives together, bent over to me and said, "Do you see verse five all bathed in yellow and glowing?"

Verse five states, *"Offer the sacrifice of righteousness and put your trust in the Lord." (KJV)* We started causing a stir to the people around us. We got very excited. There was the Lord talking to us again! He was saying be righteous and trust Me with it! His work is ongoing.

For us, this was a confirmation of what is to come. That God is pulling me out of the ordinary world I had planted myself in. God was and is taking me story by

136

story, line by line, precept by precept, to a higher calling. To be that peculiar people. To be what I am predestine to be. And that is a light on a hill that shines for God through Jesus Christ. He did not give me gifts just for my convenience and enjoyment.

God called Moses out at the age of 40. He called me at the age of 50. But, if I had my "listening ears" on better, I was really called in my youth. I am to write about all the signs and wonders that have accompanied me all throughout my life.

And to show people that God is alive and present in this day and age.

And He loves us! He wants to be involved in *our* lives! He wants you to walk in the miraculous too! He wants you to recognize when it happens to you too!

What are you predestined to be? What are the strengths He has given you?

HOME

The second year Mark and I were married, we had three people who didn't know each other, come to us and say that we would be building a home in the new year 2002. One came to us to say put our little house on the market. One came to say go out 135 South to find land. And one came to us with a builder.

We went driving out into the country to look for land for sale. Mark got a feeling to go right onto Steam Engine Road and go look around there. I wrote down before we got there, we would know the property when we saw a "for sale by owner" sign on it. The price would be $18,000.00.

We went around a corner and saw a one and a half acre plot with a "for sale by owner" sign on it and stopped. I got out and felt the Holy Spirit come upon me from the ground up. It was an absolutely beautiful piece of land. It was on top of a rolling hill that over looked a valley surrounded by rolling hills in the background. You could see for miles. We bought it for $18,000.00.

The name of the farm the land was from?
BETHLEHEM FARMS.

DADDY
Part Two

In 2005, Mark, the boys and I were still living on Mathes Road in the home we had built.

One evening after we had gone to bed, Mark woke up and said he could smell cigarette smoke. He thought maybe the boys were smoking cigarettes down stairs. They knew their mother was allergic to cigarette smoke! The funny thing was I didn't smell anything. I sniffed. Nothing.

"You stay in bed, dear and I'll go check around the house", I told him. I got up and sniffed through all the upstairs rooms, but still nothing. I went downstairs and knocked on Ben's door. He opened it and looked at me with a question on his face, "Yes Momma?" I sniffed.

"Honey, are you smoking down here?" I asked.

"No, Momma, we wouldn't smoke in the house, you are allergic, remember?" he replied. They didn't smell anything either. I told them maybe their Mark Dad had dreamed it, and I went back upstairs.

I went to our bedroom and gave a report to my husband. "No cigarettes anywhere in the house, honey." He said, "I know. It was your dad. He came to see me." This was coming out of the mouth of a very straight laced man. As far as I knew, he didn't walk this kind of walk. "What? What did my daddy have to say?"

Mark related, "Your Dad said I'm Earl. Thank you for taking care of my daughter."

Mark talked to him out loud! He replied, "Your welcome, Earl. I really love your daughter. I thank you for her."

I am in agreement with several pastors on this; we should not try to contact people who have died and gone onto their afterlife. But, if God sends them to speak to us, that's a different story. And usually, one I would write about!

LAND HO!

In 2004, a man from another state bought the 10 plus acres of land behind us. He upset several of our neighbors by planting trees to block all of our views. He told one of our neighbors he did it on purpose. We didn't buy that view, and he's not going to let us have it!

Well that was it! That was all she wrote! Well, not this she.

I started praying against him! I cried, "Lord! Don't you let this man come to our neighborhood! You send him back to where he is from! You bring us good neighbors to buy that land! Someone who loves you and will be a good neighbor to everyone!"

Four years later after we had sold our home to the Scully's, we bought the land. But that is another story!

And the first thing we did was saw down all his rotten trees too!

Share with your neighbors.

Golly.

MISSIONARIES OUT OF NOWHERE
SELLING "MATHES"
Part One

After God healed my back, He never saw fit to heal our financial situation. We finally decided to sell our home in the spring of 2006. Two days later, the housing market started its crash.

When we met with our real estate agent, I told her I only wanted to sell to a Christian. She said we couldn't do that. I replied, "Watch me." We kept up all our crosses and religious symbols inside and outside. We wanted people to know they were coming into a blessed home!

There had been miracles there, and we wanted them to continue. We took everything else down and boxed it up. Only four people came to see it in six months. The last day of the contract Mark and I started bringing up boxes from downstairs to unpack.

I said to my husband, with joy in my heart, "The only way I'd sell our home now is if God sent missionaries to our door step, and they told me God told them to buy our home!" Laughing, I told this to our agent when she came to take her signs down. Unknowingly, I had thrown a fleece before the Lord God.

Two days later our agent called us. She said, "Hold onto your hats. I've got missionaries in my office, and they think they are supposed to buy your home. They think they have been sent here by God." At that point, we couldn't even argue the price.

Although I was happy for the outcome, part of me was very sad that God had not chosen to save our home for us. So in this place in my heart, I told our agent, "I don't want to meet these people. Not even at the closing."

End of part 1.

MISSIONARIES OUT OF NOWHERE
SELLING "MATHES"
Part Two

A few weeks later, before the closing of the selling of our home, at work, I started having an arrhythmia (irregular, fast heartbeat). I told my boss and he sent me home. He thought it was stress related.

I came home to lie down to see if that would help. I wasn't home ten minutes when there was a knock at the door. There stood two adorable, smiling missionaries on my doorstep. The two people I explicitly told God I did not want to meet. I looked up to Heaven and shook my head. God knew I needed to meet my new best friends. Within ten more minutes we were fast prayer partners and friends. I ended up spending the rest of the afternoon with them. They thought they were there for a house inspection. Ha Ha! on both of us.

When they got ready to leave I walked them out to their car. I couldn't help myself. I started crying. I told them, "You will be living in the nicest house I will ever own."

Now Kaelin is a big man, well over six feet tall, barrel chested, a commanding presence, retired air force. He turned to me, pointing his arm out straight and prophesied saying, "You don't know the good God has in store for you. He is planning you a bigger and better home right now." I stood in awe and said, "From your mouth to God's ears. Let it be."

To be continued...

MOVING DAY

It's the middle of the summer of 2007 and we are living in an 800 square foot rental house. Andy, our youngest is still living with us. The house is too small to accommodate our other two sons. We only have three rooms and three rooms of furniture. We went from 3,800 square feet to 800 square feet.

I was cleaning the kitchen and went to throw away some newspaper. Immediately I got it right back out of the garbage. I felt like I was going to need this. I heard out of my head, *"You will be moving soon."* I got a call three days later from our landlord that the house down the street with an extra bedroom was coming available in three weeks. She asked if I wanted it.

I said, "Evidently so."

FINDING JEREMY
$70,000.00 REWARD

After giving up our home on Mathes, I swore I would never own another home again. Over the next several months, God worked on me and my husband's hearts. We started looking at homes and land that Spring. Occasionally, I would make calls on property I'd see in the paper.

This is how I met over the phone in 2007, a young Christian man named Jeremy. He was a realtor and a neighbor of ours when we had lived on Mathes and Nicholas Drive. I told him how we'd had to sell our home on Mathes, but it looked as if things may be turning around in the next six months. We may be able to get a home or land again. He prayed with me, both of us in tears. We prayed until I could hear two tiny little voices crying for their daddy. After we hung up, I wondered if I would ever get to talk to him again.

That Fall, the business I was with was bought, and things were looking up, at least so I thought. We started looking in earnest for land. Again from the newspaper, I made a call. It was Jeremy! I said over the phone, "Jeremy, is this you? This is Debbie, the lady who talked to you last Spring." He said, " Debbie, my old neighbor?" "Yes!" Two long lost friends who had yet to meet!

He said, "Debbie, there's land that's just come open on Nicholas, do you want to see it?" I had been down Mathis and Nicholas two weeks before that and saw land across from where our home had been. It was not what I considered a pretty piece of land. I said, "No thanks. I'm not interested in that land across from where we used to live." I hung up.

God worked on that young man's heart for twenty

minutes until he finally called me back. God would not let this go.

Before I could get a word in edgewise, he said, "Debbie! Listen to me! Do you remember the land in back of where you used to live on Mathis?" I said, "Yes. "He replied, "That is the land that is for sale!" I started laughing, "You mean the guy from Texas is selling?" Jeremy said, "Now he is from Kansas!" Still laughing, I related the story on how I prayed against him for years! How I prayed God would send someone we'd all like to be our neighbor there.

By then, we were both laughing! We bought the land eight weeks later for almost $70,000.00. Four weeks after that, my job fell through, they stopped my pay and I resigned in March of 2008.

But the good that came out of this is, our families have become very close. Jeremy and Holly allowed us to bring them to a close walk with the Lord, and we now all go to church together, and we all believe in miracles.

GOD SPEAKS

In the summer of 2007, I was on my way to work in New Albany. I was crying because the business I had tried so hard to build to help people, was being torn down by new owners fighting, and I had no say so. I knew my days there were numbered. I wasn't paid for almost a year, and I finally left eight months later.

I was crying out to God. Then, on that clear morning, I heard out loud, rolling thunder and out of it came the voice of God saying, *"I HAVE HEARD YOUR CRY. KNOW HOW MUCH I LOVE YOU."*

Instantly, complete joy came over me! I laughed with tears running down my face! This is the only time I have heard my Abba's voice so far.

CARL

In the late fall of 2007, we met a very nice man while on vacation at Walt Disney World with our children. His name was Carl Andrews. He was a Messianic Jew. It had to be a "God set up." At the time I was sick and throwing up in the back of his medical taxi cab on the way to Disney's Urgent Care Center.

Carl was driving, Mark was sitting next to him. I was in the back by myself with my head in a bucket. Carl started talking about people who have been given permission by God to call Jesus by His name, Yeshua. This was happening after I had been given permission to call Him Yeshi! Well, brothers and sisters, I started hollering in the bucket, "Halleluiah! That's me! Two years ago! Praise the Lord! God Bless God!" My head was still in the bucket, praising God! It was evident this man had found a sister, albeit sick, but nevertheless, a sister and a brother!

While I was being helped at the Care Center, Mark and Carl were exchanging information. Carl even waited to drive us back to our hotel.

The next day he called to check on me. He really was concerned. On our way home, back to Indiana, Carl called us again to make sure we were getting home okay. This time we exchanged e-mail addresses. For two and a half years we became good, close friends. It felt in my heart that I had a dad again after so many years without one. We got to know his pastor and their congregation. We met his neighbors and best friend on e-mail and over the phone. Our church pastor and our congregation prayed for Carl, his family and their church in Orlando. I had wonderful, funny, long conversations with him up to a few days before his death.

We received one last, short e-mail from his best

friend, "Carl went home."

Mark took the news better than I did. He was happy Carl went home to be with the Lord! I felt like I had just lost my second dad! I didn't know if he went peacefully, or whether he got to come home from the hospital. I could not be consoled. Mark said someone would eventually call me.

They did.

But not before I heard from Carl himself. Three days after his death, I was still crying. It was about 2:00 in the afternoon and I was ironing. I went to hang up clothes in our walk in closet. This was a very warm Spring day. While I was hanging up clothes, I said, "Oh Carl, I just want to know you are okay."

As I was walking out of the closet, I felt something cold as ice bump me against my shoulder and arm, moving past me. Pushing me out of the way! I yelped!

Then I saw in front of me a grey white mist, it walked away from me and disappeared out of my sight.

One hour later Carl's best friend called me and said Carl died very peacefully at his own home in his own bed.

Peace at last.

For me.

VISIONARY

This happened in the fall of 2007. We were having friends over for dinner. I walked to the back bedroom to call the boys for dinner. I was standing in their doorway when I felt the house jolt. Hard! It was as if something had just slammed into the earth! Not an earthquake, but a moving of the whole planet! I screamed. At this point, I did not realize I was seeing in the Spirit and not in the flesh. Within two seconds everything in my sight turned upside down, the whole room and everything. I saw Mark and Andy fall off their beds and onto the floor. I saw their beds fall down on top of them. I screamed again and bent to my knees onto the floor, not knowing which way was up. I screamed again, "Did you feel that? Did you see that?" The boys are scared now. Andy cried out, "What's wrong, Momma!" I said again, "Didn't you feel that? The earth moved!" I knew something was coming!

I worried over this. I wondered if this was prophesy for the year 2012, or whether this was a personal prophesy for me. During this time we did have a tremendous upheaval in our lives with the loss of my job and the financial stress it put us under.

That spring, Mark and I went to Mary's Farm in Southern Indiana. There was a priest there who was a visionary. I told him my experience. He said it was God's way of warning us about what was going to happen. He said God knew it would turn my world upside down.

SHEKINAH GLORY OF GOD!

My good friend of eighteen years, went home to be with the Lord the day before I started a new job. I was told I could not go to her funeral. It would be a big educational teaching day. Mark and I went to the funeral home on Tuesday evening. My friend, Diane came up and said how her calendar just "opened up" so she could go to the funeral.

I started praying. I wanted to go to the funeral too! The next night, on Wednesday, we went for a prayer service and two people told us their calendars opened up for them to be able to go to the funeral as well. I started crying.

Earlier in the day, Annie, my new friend at work, prayed with me to be able to go to the funeral. She said, "Debbie, you Catholics don't know how to pray! You don't pray the problem, you pray the solution." We held hands, and she simply said, " Thank you God that you allowed Debbie to go to her best friend's funeral."

The next morning when it was time to go to work on the day of her funeral, I cried. I cried all the way to work. I said, "Lord, I feel like the little lost lamb. You called the 99 to be there with you but not the one, not me. Why? Are you trying to tell me I am not worthy? Are they all coming home to you and I will be left standing on the outside of the gates of Heaven?"

I went to work. I walked over to my seat. Annie said to me, "You go over and talk to Tonya. See what she has to say." So I went.

Tonya said to me, " Well, we've changed all our training around. It won't be until next week. You won't have much to do Friday afternoon. I said, "Too bad Barbara isn't being buried on Friday." She said, " when is the funeral today?" I said it was from 11 am until 2 pm. She

150

asked what time I would have to leave. I said, "10:15 am." I could be back between 2:30 and 3 pm. She then said I could go!

I hugged her and cried. God went before me! He didn't forget me! Me! He came back for me! Thank you! Thank you!

It was a beautiful wonderful funeral. So many people there to say good bye to a dear lady. This was a very long day. I traveled almost 200 miles, and I was still supposed to go to the "Life in the Spirit" Seminar at St. Joe's in Corydon that night with Fr. Bernie Weber. Even though Fr. Bernie had already told me I couldn't be baptized because I missed the first class, something in me told me I had to go anyway. So I went.

He gave his talk. He told us what to expect. I sat by a lady who had been to Barbara's funeral earlier. She said to me, "Debbie aren't you already born again in the spirit?" I said, "Yes, by God. But not through this class. I feel like I'm supposed to do this as an act of obedience." She said to me, "You go up and ask Father again! Go see what he says." I said okay I would go up at the next break.

When we took a break, I went up to see Father. Fr. Bernie said to me, "Why did you miss our first class? Tell me again." I said, " Father, I did not know about it . A lady came to our prayer group and told us about this and I am the only one that came! I haven't missed one since." Then he relayed this story to me:

The night before our class, on a break in between what he was doing, God spoke to him. God said, *"ONE IS COMING TO YOU WHO THROUGH NO FAULT OF THEIR OWN, MISSED A CLASS. THEY ARE DOING MY WORK IN THE WORLD. I WANT YOU TO BAPTIZE HER."* Fr. Bernie then said to me, " I will baptize you. Promise you will come and make up the class." I said to him, "Oh, I promise! Even if I have to go to Louisville for class, I'll come!" He said next Thursday would be our last class in Corydon. We could exchange phone numbers then.

There were two priests and two lay ministers working together. They went to change into their vestments while we were on break. I went to tell the nice lady that Fr. Bernie said yes! I can be baptized! We all came back into church when the break was over. Fr. Bernie asked us to pray over them for the Holy Spirit to come down. We all stood and lifted our hands up to pray for them before we were to be prayed over.

And then I saw it. The grey smoke cloud came down through the ceiling and over the alter and the three men. It was the Shekinah glory of God! The one true Holy Spirit! I was seeing it with my own eyes! Glory! It took my breath away! I couldn't breathe! I started crying! It was Awesome!

They asked us to pray for special gifts, and he especially wanted us to pray for the gift of tongues. So I prayed. But it was not in my heart to pray for the gift of tongues that night. I prayed for three specific gifts.

1)   knowledge
2)   discernment (of the spirit)
3)   to hear a rhema word from God (spoken, out loud)

I went up when it was my time to be prayed over. The lay minister's hands felt heavy on my head. My brain felt tingly. My body felt like it was vibrating! He prayed without me telling him for the exact three things I had asked for! He placed his hands over my ears to be open to God's voice! I wailed a cry so deep!

I got back to the house at 10:30 that night. I told Mark I could hear him praying for me through the evening. He said he had been praying for me! I told him everything that had gone on!   What a wonderful full day of miracles!

RAPTURED

In March of 2009 I dreamed I was called before God. I will try to explain. I was standing back behind God who was seated in his chair. I could see me on my knees before Him crying. He said, " *I AM CALLING YOU BACK UNTO MYSELF IN THE FALL OF YOUR 54TH YEAR.* "

Weeping, I replied, " Oh, but there is so much still to do my Lord!" He stated again a little more sternly, "*I AM CALLING YOU BACK TO MYSELF IN THE FALL OF YOUR 54TH YEAR!*"

End of the dream.

There have been as many interpretations of this dream as there are people I have told it to.

JESUS

So many of the things I have experienced come out of ordinary events. I may not get a full interpretation for months or years.

In the spring of 2009 Mark and I were still renting a house, waiting on God's help to turn things around for us.

One night, our friend Kelly had come to spend the night with us. After dinner we were all sitting around in the living room talking. I must have mentioned feeling a little achy. Kelly is a massage therapist and a good prayer warrior. She volunteered to use gentle touch and prayer on my knees and elbows and where she was directed in her heart to pray over.

She stood me up in the middle of the living room and started praying for my health and wisdom. Then she sat me down on the couch and went to pray a second time over my knees, elbows, and my heart. When she got to my heart area she cried out! I immediately went into a vision. It lasted several seconds.

I looked all around me and I was no longer on my living room couch. I was in a crowd of people, dressed as they were 2,000 years ago. We were standing on a dusty dirt road. We were in a town square with earthen and sand block buildings around us. In the middle of this area was a man hunched down writing something in the dirt. He was explaining a parable, teaching the crowd. He had on what looked to be a white woolen robe tied at the waist. I could see the dirt and dust at the bottom of his hem. I could see his sandals. He had long dark hair and a beard. When he looked up, I knew it was Jesus, Yeshua of Nazareth. He pointed to a man in the crowd and motioned him over. Jesus was calling him to join him.

154

The man looked from right to left, then back at Jesus, and pointed to himself, "Me?" Jesus nodded. He stepped forward. Then I was back.

I could see normally again. Natural sound came back. Kelly and I were both hollering! Mark was impatiently waiting for an explanation of what all the commotion was about! "I've seen a vision!" I cried out. Kelly said, "Debbie, I went to touch your heart and Jesus was there!" She had seen something too.

I told them what I had seen. She thought it meant I was an apostle of Jesus in another lifetime. I said, "I don't think so. I think it means He is in my heart, and He is calling me to be an apostle now! I am to listen to His teachings and do what He tells me." Kelly went on to say, "He is calling you to do something big!"

I am only now, a year out from this, following what He has been trying to tell me all this time. Write His book. Be obedient. Be an example. Be an apostle. Okay.

THREE VISIONARY DREAMS

From the fall of 2009 through Christmas time, I had three visionary dreams.

I woke up one morning hearing a heavenly song singing over and over, "I will turn my back on you no more." Things felt in my spirit as though they were "ramping up". Listen and write everything down. You are going to need it. Prepare. Tell everything you've seen and heard. I'm telling.

THE WEDDING INVITATION

I dreamed Mark and I were at my Momma's, and we were all getting ready to go to a wedding. I went to walk over to our apartment in a high rise because it was close by. Along the way a man passed me by, jogging. He looked very strong. As he passed me he said, "Hello." I responded with a "hello" and a smile back. Ahead of me, he stopped a girl passing by and hugged her. Another girl went walking by, and I could see him stop and hug her as well. This time he looked back at me grinning and said, " I only hug the pretty ones." I laughed and said, "So that's how it is!" I caught up with him and ran around him and started up the stairs to our apartment building.

He came running up behind me, grabbed me around my waist and hauled me up the stairs with him! When he got to the top of the stairs, he sat down and sat me on his lap! We were both laughing! I took off my glasses to look at him. He was very handsome. His eyes danced as he asked, " Are you coming to my wedding?" I smiled back and said, "Yes, I'll come to your wedding. Let me go get my husband. He gets off at 3 pm and we'll

156

come." He got up and ran back down the stairs saying, "I'll tell them to save you a place!"

I went and got Mark and Momma. We got in the car and headed for the church. On the way, a tractor trailer caused a big wreck a few cars in front of us. A tree was hit and it fell on our car. We got out to look at the damage. Then the car rolled out into the other lane and got hit by another car and demolished it! I thought Mark was still in the car! He was standing in back of me. I looked behind me and asked, "Are you a ghost?" He replied sheepishly, "No. I forgot to set the brake." I said, "We have to get to church! We are going to be late!"

A lady from a nearby bank came out to see if everyone was okay. We started talking to her. She asked if we knew any book keepers, they needed one. I told her I had eight years experience. She wanted me to come interview right then. I had to choose between working or going to the wedding.

Then I woke up.

HEALING TOUCH

Again, I was dreaming. Mark and I were on vacation. We were in a hotel. We had a blond male child about 24 years old. He was sick. The doctor came and gave him a shot and said to feed him meat.

We went to bed in the dream. I felt the Holy Spirit come over me. The palms of my hands began to burn like fire! I could see them red hot! I woke Mark up in the dream and showed him "healing hands". The mark of the Stigmata. The gift of healing.

I heard God ask me if I knew what to do now. I said, "Build a home?" He cried out, "*Think bigger! I have bigger things for you to do! Spread My Gospel!*" "Oh, yes, Lord, I know!" I responded quickly.

Then I awoke. The palms of my hands were still hot.

I AM AN ANGEL OF THE LORD!

I dreamed we were just finishing up building a home on our land. We were setting a few things on the fire place mantle in the living room. I could see around the room. The walls were white with wooden trim. We had hard wood floors.

Myself, Mark and friends Holly and Jeremy were there. The guys were deciding where to put the furniture. Their little girls were running around. Our boys were there deciding which bedroom was whose.

The front door opened and a man in blue jeans and a jacket came in. He walked over to me. I turned around and looked at him. I did not recognize him.

He said, *"I am an angel of the Lord."* He had short wavy brown hair and brown eyes. He looked like he had been in a "tussle". I said, "Speak."

He went on saying, ***"The Lord God will hold off judgement for a short time so you can have a time of joy, peace, and to prosper. Then the Great Judgement will come upon all. Get ready."***

My reply to him, "Be it so."

Does this mean upon all the earth? Or just me?
I am not sure.
Either way, pray for mercy for us all.

GOD'S PROTECTION

I went to Aunt Jackie's funeral with my good friend Kelly. It was really her Aunt Jackie, but everybody called her Aunt Jackie. My husband, Mark, could not come due to work. Kelly in a nice pants outfit and I in a black dress looked very nice to represent our families.

While Mark was at work, about 9am, he started being attacked by the devil in his head. He felt that I was in trouble, and that Kelly's cousin was going to talk me into leaving Mark and cheat on him! He started praying for me. This was a huge attack in his head.

About 9:30 that morning in the coffee room at the funeral home, I was in getting a cup of tea. I was standing there talking to a lady when Kelly's cousin came in. He started hollering and cussing! I looked up to see what was wrong with him! He was looking at me and said, "You clean up real good. Real good."

I could tell immediately his thoughts were not pure at all. I said, "Stop it! Stop it right now! Do not curse or swear again. I am sure somewhere in you, you mean it as a compliment, but stop it!" He said, " Well, can I say Jesus?" I said, "Yes, Jesus is good."

God stopped the attack. He did not speak to me again the rest of the day. God gave me the words to stop whatever was going on in his head.

When Kelly's little brother came in the room, he told him, "Don't even start. She's married." Her little brother replied, "When's that ever stopped us?" Her cousin then said, "This one is a lady." End of conversation. He left me alone the rest of the day also.

Later that afternoon when I got back home, I called my husband to let him know I made it back safely. He was so glad I called him. He had worried all day.

160

He told me about what had been going on in his head and how he had been praying for me. Then I told him what happened. After I hung up the phone, I went right to my husband's work, and we held each other thanking God everything turned out well.

SISTERS

At Believer's Fellowship 6pm service, on the second Sunday in April 2010, Pastor Fred taught on the gifts of the Holy Spirit of God. In Hebrew it is named the Ruach HaKodesh, and in Greek it is Pneuma. In English, it is breath of God or wind of God. He especially taught on healing, wisdom and knowledge, and all the different ways they come such as; dreams, interpretations, visions, words of knowledge. At the end of the service, Fred prayed over us to receive these gifts. While he was praying over us, I was praying for my family. I had two family members just days out of the hospital, two family members very, very ill, and two family members out of jobs. Well, saints, that's all my immediate family! Then there's us and our boys! At first I was asking for money to help change situations. But then, I changed my prayer. I asked God to give me anything to take to them like faith, healing, a word, prophesy, hope, or peace. I started crying.

In response, I felt heat come up in me, then down into my heart. I knew the Holy Spirit was there, and He was searching my heart! I cried even harder! I wanted Him to feel what I felt!

Afterwards, I was talking with brother Bill and Lisa. Bill prophesied that this night, we would all have dreams and prophesy, write them down and share them with the church. That night, when Mark and I were getting ready for bed, we promised each other we would wake each other whenever we had dreams through the night. Well, most of the night, we had busy dreams, we were helping someone or working. In the morning, after Mark got ready and went off to work, I fell back asleep and this is what I dreamed.

162

I was back in the home where I grew up. Daddy was there, me and Ron were getting ready for school and Momma was in the kitchen. On the bed in my bedroom was a letter in Momma's handwriting addressed to my dad and our address on it. In it was a card and some money. What I thought in my heart was "Gee, I could really use some money, do you think daddy will let me have some of his?"

I went and told dad he had left a letter with money in my room. We were in the living room talking. Ron noticed there were two big cracks in the living room window. We could see it giving way. Dad ran to one end of the house, and Ron and I ran back to the bedrooms. Immediately a tall man came and fixed the window better than ever. We all went to see it and looked outside. It was cold and snowing. I said, "Oh, I forgot it was winter." I walked back to the bedroom, and the letter was still on my bed. This time it had more money in it. Daddy said, " Here, if this is what you want, take it, take it all." I said, "Oh daddy, don't be mad. I don't want all your money!" Then I woke up.

I woke up about 8:15 that morning and started writing the dream down. When I got to the part about the snow, I knew it meant something. I thought, "Pastor Ivie will know what this means. I'll ask her the next time I talk to her."

Pastor Ivie had relocated to South Carolina to be with her children and do God's mission work there.

I started fixing my breakfast and ate my last bite at 9:45 am. The phone rang. It was Ivie's number! She was calling me! When I picked up the phone there was nothing but static on the line. I knew immediately satan was trying to stop our conversation. I started praying. This time she got through. She said to me, "I am on my break at school and I only have five minutes, but the

Lord told me it was important for me to call you right now!" I told quickly of what Pastor Fred had preached, what Bill prophesied, and what I dreamed. This was what she interpreted for me from the Holy Spirit:

" *Snow is two fold. It means cleansing, possibly from a struggle. Winter is the season you are coming out of. Money represents new beginnings. You are coming into spring. The tall smiling man was Jesus, He makes everything new. He fixes everything all better than it was.*

Then she prophesied:

You may be living in a subdivision now, but I still see a nice house on your land. You will rent or sell this home to be debt free in your next home. You will be able to build debt free on your land so that your income will be free to be seed money to share the gospel and to tithe. To give to others in need.

I thanked her for her time and obeying God to call me. Then we hung up.

Has God asked you to walk something out in the natural you can't see either? Sometimes it is hard for us too. That is why it is called faith.
Keep walking.
I am.

DREAMS

GLEANING

The road by our land was paved. We had a nice brick home. Across the street was a very nice house, a million dollar home! A couple of famous preachers lived there who had just moved in. I baked them some home made bread, and Mark and I went to introduce ourselves. We were asked into their living room, and we looked out their picture window. In the very back of their land, way off, was a factory, disturbing their view. The message I was given immediately was this:

"Glean what is good, for all churches in My name have some good in them, and disregard the rest - that which is man made opinion and not God's.

A COVENANT HOUSE

I was on a country road with my oldest son, Ben, as a boy. There was a covered swinging seat. I laid down on it as Ben went to play in the field. I was crying. I cried and cried, " Please God, I don't want to go to hell. I love you. I am sorry for anything I have ever done wrong. Please forgive me. I love only you! Please send me a sign you have heard me."

Suddenly, a delivery truck pulled up and a man got out. He said to me, " I have something for you." There were two things. One was a baby bottle with milk in it for Ben. The other was a piece of paper. It was a contract. A covenant contract between God and me. (And mine).

It read:
I AM PROTECTED.
I AM HERE FOR GOD'S WORK.
I WORK FOR GOD.

I felt peace come over me. The interpretation came - the journey has started.

This was the end of April 2010 when God started ministering to people's heart's that I was to write for the Lord.

We need to be good listeners. The more you read your bible the better you will become at hearing God's voice. He will speak to you out of your own head with His words. He will guide you and keep you in all your ways.

166

WILMA

In the summer of 2010, it came to me to ask God to order my steps each morning. Every day, everywhere became a mission field for me. Within three hours of first asking this to be, God lined up three missions to do for me the next week! I did not go to them, they came to me!

By the first week of September, I was getting used to being called on to do good deeds, be an angel to someone or be a witness to everyday miracles. One morning I asked God for a second time, a simple question, "What do you want of me, Lord?" ***OBEDIENCE.*** Pretty plain. Okay. Order my steps, Lord.

Are you aware that when you are helping someone, doing a good deed or going that extra mile for a cause, that this could very well be your mission field? Even going to the grocery store can turn into an act of obedience. How?

Just like this...

It was not a particularly splendid fall. The hottest summer on record starting in May did not end record heat days until almost the middle of October. We were ten inches lacking in precipitation. The weather people called this a drought. Our farmers called it hell.

By the end of the third full week of October, the temperature was a nice reasonable 80 degrees. Mark and I were having a leisurely Sunday morning jaunt to the grocery store. He had taken several days off to do mission work for people. Yard work for one, concrete work for another and hosting a yard sale for three families one of which was us!

That morning in the grocery store, I really didn't expect to be called out. My thinking was we've been really useful and busy for the Lord lately, I was sure this was to be a restful day. But order my steps Lord. When I say my steps that could and usually does mean my husband's steps as well.

In the grocery we saw several people we knew, and we stopped to chat. We even made a new friend or two. We started down the bread aisle and the spirit of tongues fell on me. I felt the Holy Spirit come and quicken my spirit. I told Mark and he just smiled.

We went to get in line to pay for our groceries. Miss Wilma, who we've known for many years, directed us to our checkout line. I turned around to thank her, and she was glowing! I smiled because I knew the Holy Spirit of God was up to something! I said to her, "Would you like a hug?" Without saying anything she nodded her head yes. I hugged her and my spirit moved.

Something's wrong.

I looked her in the eyes, she still stood there smiling at me, not moving. I said to her, "Do you need me to pray for you?" She nodded her head yes, still not saying a word. She couldn't, she was too close to tears.

My husband was busily checking out our groceries. I put down my pen and grocery list on top of my purse. "Watch these honey, I'm praying!" I told him. He was not the least bit surprised.

I took Wilma by the hand and got close to her. There were people in line behind us. They waited. I asked, "What do we need to pray for?" She replied, "My husband has cancer. They operated and said they got it all but I'm afraid." I replied, " Well, that's two spirits you have to be rid of, the spirit of cancer on your husband and the spirit of fear on you! Okay, let's go before the Lord!" I started praying. We called on a mighty God to minister to Wilma and her beloved for a healing and peace and for any spirits not of God to vanish and leave. A two minute prayer. We finished in Jesus name. I hugged her

168

again and told her "I love you".

I would be looking for a good praise report from her.

Then back to this world's cares. Groceries are paid for, and my husband was patiently waiting. The next customer was ready to go. On the way out to the car I was jumping!

"Do you know why I get excited when God uses me to do His ministry work?" I asked my husband. He just listened for my explanation. " Because He knows I am here!" I was yelling and smiling! I was full of the Holy Spirit.

At this Mark laughed. He started to preach to me. "Honey, you have heard God's voice out of thunder tell you He loves you. You have been directed into the bible by your name and He showed you He loves you. Yes, He knows you are here!"

This led me to wonder. Is the reason He knows I am here, besides the fact He made me, because I am moveable. "Go here", I go here. "Go there", I go there. "Do this", Yes Sir, *sometimes* without question or argument!

I am not perfect, but I know and serve the One who is!

Are you moveable too?

BREAKTHROUGH!

In this dream Andy, our son, Mark, my husband, and myself along with many, many others were in a telling dream. It was the battle between good and evil. We were fighting evil.

Usually when I dream of battling the devil, I dream we are running or fighting and saying the name of Jesus trying to over come whatever we are in. This time I had wisdom, I could see evil in people, places and events. The devil was fighting me in all these. But this time I was going after him!

I used the name of Jesus, Yeshua, with power and authority. I was physically fighting the devil when I heard God say, ***"STOP FIGHTING! USE MY POWER!"***

Then I walked up to the devil and put the sign of the cross on his forehead. I said, "Yeshua, Yeshua, Yeshua. At that name you have to bow." I could feel the power of the Holy Spirit in me, out of me, and over flowing the situation.

The devil stopped and looked at me. He could see I had wisdom from God. He could no longer fool me or hinder me. The devil looked like an adversary.

When I woke up, I knew I had been in a physical battle. My lungs, back and right hip hurt. In the dream, I had thrown satan over my right hip. He tried to take my life. As the song says, "Victory in Jesus!"

TALKING WITH GOD

Mark and I had decided one afternoon in August of 2010 to take a drive out highway 111 to see his old home where he grew up. When we drove past the tire store, I got a warning. I should have told my husband, Mark, but I did not. We went out 111 and the right front tire gave out. We didn't have a blow out, even though we should have. No harm to us. But Mark couldn't get the spare off the truck. We started walking and praying. Not three minutes later a couple picked us up and drove us from Elizabeth to Corydon. They would not take any money.

We took our car to get the tire and then to the tire store in Clarksville. We had $128.00 in the bank. The new tire costs us $127.10. We had ninety cents left!

When we got back to the truck with the new tire, Mark was putting it on, and I was singing praise to God while sitting in my car. As I was sitting there and singing and praising, my whole head felt on fire! Tingling! It came all the way down to my chin and lips were tingling and numb. I started praising and singing in tongues.
It was not the same sentence over and over, but a whole conversation.

The Holy Spirit was with me, and I was talking before God! I was not afraid, I was calm. Joyful tears. Mark came and prayed thanksgiving and glory to God with me!

HOLLY

At five foot nothing (I don't care what she tells you!) and just over 100 pounds, Holly is petite. But, her spirit is ten feet tall, and I'm pretty sure she is bullet proof. She is formidable where it counts! Ask her husband, Jeremy, he'll tell you.

We have been fast friends for over three years at this writing. My husband and I had the privilege of guiding and renewing their relationship with Jesus Christ. In our hearts, they are our children too. Their children are our practice grandchildren. We spend many evenings until it becomes early morning at their home engrossed in biblical understanding. The growth we have seen from this young couple is phenomenal.

Holly and God are writing buddies.

Jeremy and God are working buddies.

One evening the first week of September 2010 Holly told me of an encounter she had with God. She had gone to bed praying out loud, then in her spirit, then in her dreams. It was as if there was a presence with her responding to her prayers of love for God Himself.

As she was waking up early that morning she found herself surrounded by a grey sparkly cloud. This is the Shekinah Glory of God! He Himself has come down from Heaven to be with her in response to the love she has for Him! She said it was amazing. She was not sleepy but entirely alert. There was pure love and peace surrounding her. No care or concern could enter her being. This earthen world had passed away and she had become a "New Jerusalem."

This is one of the moments you live for. It takes your breath away.

She was and is the bride of Christ.

GOD WRITES

Well, the calendar on the wall said the season was fall, the second week of October, 2010, but the thermometer outside kept breaking record after record of hottest year ever in Kentuckiana.

A dear friend, Kelly, had come to stay with us for a few days to celebrate my birthday. We had stayed up celebrating the Lord's wonderful mercy till a late bedtime. I was very surprised when I woke up at 4 am and couldn't go back to sleep. I figured this must be a good time to have some quiet time with the Lord. For an hour until 5 am I ministered to God Himself. I wanted Him to know in my heart of hearts, how much I love Him. How much He means to me. I didn't want anything. No long list. Although at a minute's notice I can sure make one up! But how far is that from any of us? I cried, thanking Him over and over for loving me, "And, please, I know it's taken a long time to see clearer what You are doing in my life, but please don't give up on me! I'll keep trying!" I threw kisses in the air and asked the angels to carry them to my God in Heaven. I reached my arms out as in a big bear hug!

I nodded off to sleep about 5 am with a stuffy nose from crying so much. At 6 am I got a reply from God. I woke up again feeling a tremendous urge to open my Bible. I sat up, took it off my night stand and asked the Lord to guide me.

Well, I went all the way to the back pages of the concordance. I thought, "I must've got it wrong! What am I doing in the back in the names in the Bible?" There at the top of the page standing out is my name in Hebrew! *Devorah.*

He is calling me by my name!!

173

Then quickly I turned to somewhere in Psalms. It was very early in the morning, I had had three hours sleep and I only remembered what He showed me!
On the page I stopped at is one line circled and one line underlined.

So the message went like this:

DEVORAH
I LOVE YOU   (Circled)
I AM THE GOD OF ALL (underlined)

A personal love letter from God!

Later that morning, the door bell rang, and no one was there. I called out, "Only the Holy Spirit of the living God is welcome here!"

In the afternoon, Kelly and I were speaking about angels and the lights blinked as if in agreement with us!

SHIFT IN THE UNIVERSE
RESTORATION

I dreamed Mark and I were back in our rental house on Main Street. We were in bed in the dream. I was still awake and talking to the Lord telling Him my heart's desires.

I talked about how I missed being able to do the things we used to do. How we could help people at the drop of a hat. Having our friends over for prayer groups at our home on Mathes Road. I missed our big home. I missed having money. We didn't even have grocery money at the time. "That's not the way it is supposed to be, being Your children! I miss being with You and in Your blessings!" Then I asked God to restore us with my whole heart.

The next instant the room started to slowly shift counter clockwise 45 degrees to 90 degrees. Then it came back. I saw it just like I saw the vision of everything turning upside down. But this was gentle. This had a good feeling about it, like everything was being restored. I started calling out to Mark, " Mark! Honey! God has done something! He's restoring us! Restoration! There has been a shift in the universe! I felt it happen! I still feel it! Mark wake up!"

This was in early October of 2010

When I woke up I felt in my soul, accomplished. How?

That was the week I started writing this book.

Tell my story so the readers will know how to tell their stories.

JEREMY'S PROPHESY

We have many friends who walk in the supernatural. We know many pastors who walk in the supernatural, too. Jeremy just happens to be one of them.

One warm fall evening, he came over for dinner. We had picked up their children off the school bus and brought them over to our home for dinner until he or Holly came home from work. We made enough dinner so Jeremy could eat when he got there too. We all had bible study to go to later that evening. He was finishing up dinner when he looked across the table at me and began to speak, " A few days ago I was thinking about you and the book you are writing. I heard God say that it was already done. It just needs to be organized."

Truth.

HOPE FOR THE NEW YEAR!

A few days after Christmas 2010, we found ourselves going over to the Ward's to celebrate "Holly's birthday/Christmas/New Year's Eve eve/ party. A very nice dinner was served as always. And afterwards, gifts were exchanged.

Their little girls scampered around. Mark and Jeremy sat back in their chairs and lounges. Holly and I talked up a storm as usual.

At one point in the conversation, Jeremy was speaking about the new year and his feelings of apprehension about just starting a new job and how well things would go. About that time, I saw a beautiful color of green all around him, like a halo. After making sure of what I was seeing, I opened the front of my bible to see what exactly that color meant. It meant healing and harvest. I looked up at Jeremy again. Yep, it was still there. All around him.

I told everyone what I was seeing and the interpretation that had come with it. Healing and harvest were coming to this household. Lay aside all fears.

I saw smiles all around the room.

What a beautiful color.
What a beautiful message.
Hope for the new year.

INTERMISSIONS

SINGING

GLORY TO GOD THE LAMB
HE CAME TO ME JUST AS I AM
ALLELUIA, PRAISE THE LORD
IT'S JUST AS HE HAD FORETOLD
GLORY TO HIM THAT SITS ON THE THRONE
WE ARE CALLED TO BE HIS OWN!

Song given to me upon awakening   Fall 2010

When the devil reminds you of your past,
remind him of the future God has in store
for you!

OUT OF THE MOUTHS OF BABES

One day I was singing before the Lord while I was doing housework and cooking. Our youngest son, Andy, was in the kitchen area too. He was in his mid-teens at the time. I spoke to him with my heart. I said, "Son, isn't it a wonderful time to be alive in this age of miracles?"

The wise Solomon replied, "Momma, it has been the age of miracles since God made the universe."

Sometimes, children have to put us in our place - the teachable place!

SHORT STORY

When my friend Joan was four years old, she got lost in a cave on a farm in Southern Indiana. Living out in the country, that is not a hard thing to do. What she remembered the most was a man in white helping her and guiding her out of the cave.

Then he disappeared.

An angel or the King of the angels, it really doesn't matter.

I told you this was a short story!

MINDLESS KNOWLEDGE

When I was 14 years old, I caught a flu. I was at home sick on the couch on a beautiful day. My little brother, Ron, had gone for a walk to the store. Momma was home taking care of me.

While lying on the couch, I was shown Ron at the store buying me my favorite candy, Willy Wonka Oompa's, to cheer me up.
It did.

I never gave it a thought as to why I could see this, or that it might be considered slightly unusual to be able to see in this manner.

I never figured I'd be telling anyone.

GOD WILL SHOW US THINGS
FOR NO REASON AT ALL

While we were living on Mathis road with our boys, one day I was having lunch with Pastor Ivie Dennis. I was serving her lunch and all of a sudden she had white hair. Since I have known her she has always had dark hair. She noticed my puzzled look and asked what was wrong.

I told her what I thought had just occurred. I said, "Oh Ivie, the Lord just showed me the future! He showed me us in twenty years sitting here, still friends, having lunch!" She asked me how I knew it was twenty years from then. I said, "It was evident, pastor. You had a head full of white hair."

She laughed and laughed. She replied to me, "Oh my dear sister, God is not showing you the future. He is telling on me in the present! This is not my natural hair color. I am all white headed now! I color my hair!"

I joined in her laughter.

You may be able to fool a cover girl, but you can't fool God.

Part Three

EVERYDAY MIRACLES

"And it shall come to pass in the last days, saith God, I will pour out of My Spirit upon all flesh:
and your sons and daughters shall prophesy, and your young men shall see visions, and your old men shall dream dreams.
And on my servants and on my handmaidens I will pour out in those days of my Spirit; and they shall prophesy."

Acts 2: 17-18

PROLOGUE

EVERYDAY MIRACLES

It is always so nice when we see God bless us in everyday occurrences. There is no such thing as coincidence. People, things, items, homes, land, cars, etc., come to you when it is their time, when you need them. This is open to all of us as we are open to receive it. I believe angels are on the ready to help us everyday!

Did you ever think of seeing yourself as an angel in waiting, waiting to help someone out of a spot? Following marching orders?

Being at the right place at the right time with an obedient heart is not a coincidence. It is manifesting God's work on earth. Remember, God walks to and fro the earth seeking who will.

Will you?

I call this section everyday miracles because miracles occur everyday!

LIGHTNING

I worked for a bank at the corner of 4th and Ormsby in Louisville, Kentucky when I was 22 years old. I worked day shift in the operations center from 1978 until spring of 1984. Down the street from us, past a light, was a little shopping area. There was another bank, a drug store, a flower shop, a restaurant, etc. At that time, we got a one hour lunch break each day. Sometimes, some of us girls would walk down the street to get lunch together. Some days, I would run errands by myself.

This particular day I was on an errand. I didn't realize, of course, whose errand I was actually running.

I was on my way back to the bank, coming to an intersection, when I saw a little old lady in distress. She was clinging to the light pole at the cross walk. She was crying out, "Help me! Anybody! I can't walk by myself!"

So many people were walking right past her, not seeing or caring about her! It broke my heart! I ran to her crying, "Here I am! I'll help you!" She clung to me right away. Her tiny frame sagging against me. She said, " Oh, thank you! I couldn't hold out much longer! I need to get across two streets and go to my bank."

Off we went at a turtle's pace! Of course we couldn't make it across the street at the amount of time given by the stop light. I bravely held my arm out in the stop position at the oncoming traffic. Everyone stopped. And waited. No one blew their horn for us to hurry. When we arrived at our destination, the ladies at her bank took over for me.

Mission gently accomplished. Open eyes, open ears, respond. When we help the least of these, we help Jesus Himself.

LIGHTNING STRIKING TWICE

They say history repeats itself. Could it be that way in our own families lives as well? What's the odds of lightning striking twice? Another family member in the same situation at the exact same age his mother was when she heard a cry out.

Ben, our oldest son, back in the fall of 2007, when he was 22, was driving on a busy road in Louisville, Kentucky. He was stopped at a red light, not in a particular hurry. He looked past the light and saw a little old man, hitch hiking. Ben watched as car after car passed him by. His heart cried out! Oh no! Please, someone help him! No one stopped to help or even give him a look.

The light turned green and off sped Ben to the rescue to his new destination! He pulled in the drive past the old man and jumped out of his car and yelled exuberantly, "Hey old dude! I'll pick you up! Where do you need to go?"

Now I want you to see what this elderly gentleman saw. He saw a silver Mitzubishi Eclipse sports car pull up, a tall dark handsome young man jump out of the car, smiling like he just found his lost grandpa.

Ben related the first thing the 86 year old man did was drop his jaw, eyes wide, and pointed to himself, "Me?" "Yeah, I'm talking to you." Some every day "angels" are very handsome!

Ben helped his new acquaintance in his car and introduced himself. The old man needed to go to the bank and the grocery. Wonderful! A new journey!

The poor dear was so flustered at first he couldn't remember which bank was his. With gentle patience and a good sense of humor all was accomplished.

192

Ben took him home. The old man asked him to stay and visit a while. He shared some of his story with Ben. They talked for awhile and then said their good bye's.

Ben later that day thanked God for blessing him to be of service.

Open eyes, open ears, respond. What a heart. God calls us all to service.

All who will.

Will you?

GOD'S LAUGHTER

While we were living in our home on Mathes Road, after the healing of my back, and I was back to helping people with their medicine needs, I was getting ready for the day. I hopped out of the tub and was singing to the Lord, and being a whole lot of silly.

All of a sudden, it occurred to me to ask God a question. So I asked, "Lord, did you mean to make me this way?" As God is my witness, I heard laughter! Loud! Inside and outside of my head!

You see, He hears us. He knows us the way we know our children.

My reply to this Heavenly eruption? I blushed and said, "Okay, okay! I get it!" The answer when I recall it, still brings me to a joyful place in my heart and spirit.

Have you ever made God laugh?
I'm believing you have!

194

MINDLESS HELP

My husband, Mark, is a bench jeweler. That means he is a craftsman. He can build, repair, or clean anything in the art of jewelry. His busiest season is from mid-November to December 24th. From Thanksgiving to Christmas Eve. I probably get to see him two whole days. I call myself the "Christmas Widow". He hates it when I say that!

Christmas Day is shared with many a family and friends. But, December 26th is our day! We ask for the same gifts every year, cash or tickets to the movies or restaurant cards to eat out on. That way we get a whole day to play, shop, eat and go see movies all on other peoples' nickels. It's a wonderful treat, and we have a blast together.

Mark has always said I don't pay enough attention to my surroundings. December 26th, 2006 is nothing unusual for me. We had just finished lunch at a nice restaurant in the shopping mall. I was just walking and talking away as we walked toward the curb to go to the car. All of a sudden without missing a beat in the conversation, I left my husband's side, and walked over to a van at the side of the curb.

There was a little girl trying to close a big van door. Inside the van was the mother at the steering wheel, two other little children strapped into their seats, and an elderly grandmother sitting in her seat by the door, trying to help her close it from her seat. Again, I was in full conversation with my husband. I took a break to say, "I got this." as I picked the little girl up and put her in the front seat, closed her door, and then closed the big van door for the family.

I remember hearing "thank you! thank you!"

Saints, I tell you, I did not know what I was doing until I was closing the second door!

I went back over to my husband's side still "jawing" away. He was looking at me intently. I stopped and said, "What?" He replied with a smile, " How did you know they needed help?" I replied, "I didn't know. I didn't see them until I was over helping them." By this time, he was smiling even bigger, "That's my little helper angel."

Isn't it interesting that my natural eyes were closed but my spiritual eyes were open, and available for God to use. Halleluiah!

My prayer for you?
Be open, too.

FEEDING THE POOR

The reason I called this an every day miracle is because this should be an every day miracle in someone's life. It just happened to be mine and his.

I was having a busy day with lots of housework and errands to do. In between breaths I called out, "Order my steps, Lord!"

On the way to run errands, I again said, "Lord, allow me to touch a life today in a positive way! Thanks!" I went to the grocery and the shoe store. My last errand was to the local grocery store to pick up a pair of sun glasses. It was a very hot day during the record breaking summer of 2010. I finished up and headed out the door wondering why God didn't send someone for me to give a kind word or to pray over. I walked out of the store in a hurry.

A young man was sitting on the bench outside the doorway and mumbled something to me as I walked past. I hardly noticed him. I stopped. Confused, I walked back to him. His head was bowed, his shoulders hunched down as if in despair. I said, "I'm sorry. I didn't hear you. What did you say?"

He looked up at me. His face was beet red and he was sweating. He stammered, "Could you spare some change?" He looked as if he had been out in the heat for a long time. The sum total I had on me was 38 cents. I told him, "I'm so sorry. All I have is 38 cents." He hung his head down.

I started to walk away. I heard very clearly and loud in my spirit, *"Ask him when is the last time he has eaten."* I turned back around and spoke to him again, "Young man, when was the last time you ate?" He responded with a small amount of hope in his voice,

"A nice person bought me a drink!" He pointed to it by his feet. "I was so thirsty", he declared. Again I said, "When was the last time you had anything to eat?" He put his head down again, "Yesterday."

As the mother of three sons that statement about broke me. I knew all we had was $15.00 in the bank but that child was getting a meal! "Get up boy!", I cried. "Get out of this heat! We are going into the sandwich shop and get you some lunch!" I wasn't asking him, I was telling him! He obediently followed me inside the store.

I bought him the biggest sandwich, biggest drink, chips and dessert they had! I listened to his story, informed him that the local police department may be able to help him get a ticket back home to his mother. Then I prayed for him.

The next time I went to the grocery, he was not there. In my heart, I believe he got to go home.

Stay safe, young man.

If it was in your power to keep someone from going hungry, wouldn't you help too? I knew you would.

So does God.

FEED MY SHEEP

It was a vibrant October day. Mark and I had been invited to eat dinner at Aunt Mary's. After Mark got off work, we went to pick up Mom and meet our youngest son and his wife there. Mark's sister, Susan was already there helping with the meal.

As usual, Aunt Mary had set a beautiful table and cooked more than enough to eat. We all sat down, gathered hands and Mark gave thanks to Jesus for plenty at all our tables. The fine meal and conversation commenced! The time went quickly, and we are all too soon cleaning the table up and doing dishes.

At the end of the evening, Mary asked if we would like to take home some leftovers. I told her no thanks, we were just fine. She asked again and again. I finally said, "Why yes, thank you, Aunt Mary. We'd be happy to have some ham and biscuits to take with us."

On the way home, we stopped in at Ben's, our oldest son, to show Grandma his new apartment. When we got there, I picked up the food to take it in to Ben. Mark looked at me and I shrugged my shoulders. "I dunno", I said, "I just feel like I'm supposed to take this food in to them."

We knocked on the door. Ben greeted us with a smile. When he saw me with food in my hands, he got very happy! He related the story that had just unfolded.

The meal he and Amanda had made together, turned out sour. It tasted like plastic! Five minutes before we arrived, they sat down, took their first bites, and said "yuck!" Ben said out loud, "God, what are we going to do about this?"

That was when I knocked on the door with food in my hands. God answered his cry out right away!

For parents, who love the Lord and put Him first, the blessings of their household, extend to their children!

"ST. VINCENT DE _PAUL_"
PAUL BENJAMIN'S GIFT
Part One

When the boys were little, we received help from several different organizations at Christmas and other times. The boys and I always said if God ever gave us a large financial blessing, we would give back to the ones who helped us the most. God remembers the intentions of our hearts.

Thanksgiving week of 2010, I had to have a root canal so no turkey for me. Mark was sitting on the couch with me, watching me recuperate. We got a phone call from our son, Ben. He had a question for his Momma!

He was just getting off work in the local mall when he saw a donation box for winter coats for the needy. He had on his good leather jacket. It looked nice on him. It was cold out and he needed it. Why, then, won't this feeling that he was supposed to give it to this organization go away? He was talking to me and explaining his predicament as he was walking towards the exit.

I quietly listened. He finally said when he got to the door to go outside, "I have to give up my coat, don't I, Momma?" I replied, "Son, maybe God has something better for you in mind. I am sure there is a reason you have to give to this particular donation box. Whose is it?" "I don't know, Momma," he replied, " I better go back and see."

We talk casually as he walked back to the donation center. I said, "Look for a sign on the side of the box. It will tell you who you are donating to." When he got there, he read to me, "It's the St. Vincent De Paul Society." It hit us both at the same time. Ben still remembered when they came with gift certificates to buy groceries and supplied us with coats the first year we moved back to Indiana from Florida.

In the middle of the mall where he worked, he started crying, tears rolling down his face. I cried with him over the phone. This was why he had to give to this box! God remembered the intentions of our hearts. Still crying, he took his coat off, now, not caring if he got cold or how good that coat had looked on him.

He went on to tell me he had other clothes and toys that were in his trunk needing to be donated somewhere. He asked me if he wrote a letter of explanation, did I think they would accept these gifts. I told him if anyone knew a family in need of his donations, it would be these people. He wrote a lovely letter of explanation to them and placed lovingly all his gifts in the manger, I mean in the box.

And in his trunk, he found an old hooded sweatshirt warm enough to get him home. Every need was met.

Baby Jesus would have been pleased.

PAUL BENJAMIN'S GIFTS
Part Two

Remember how I told Ben maybe God had better in mind for him than what he was giving up? The next week, Ben's final week working at the department store, a beautiful medium sized upgraded pea coat came in. It was the only medium they got in. It was a $200.00 coat that Ben could buy for $65.00! Sold American!

It is the nicest coat he has ever owned.

God always gives back to you more than you can give away in His service.

Thank you, God, for taking care of our sons. You see, He is restoring their lives one piece at a time, just as He is restoring mine and yours too.

COOKING WITH DAVID

This is for all of you who think that God isn't in the little everyday details of our lives, that those kinds of things don't matter to Him. He is a big God and deals with only big issues in our lives. To that I say, "Oh yeah? Read this!"

In the early fall of 2010, when it's still so hot outside you could fry an egg anywhere, I went grocery shopping. Yes, I asked God to order my steps on that day. When I ask this I expect to be helping someone else along their way,. Not usually to be a benefit to myself. So, I walked down the aisle of goods to bake with. I got almost to the end of the aisle. I felt strongly in my spirit to pick up the molasses. As if I were going to need it. At that point I was not thinking about baking anything! I said out loud, "Lord! I am not baking anything! It's too hot outside to be turning on an oven!" I physically could not walk past the molasses. "Okay, it's not in my budget, but I'll buy it. I hope You know what You are doing, and I hope I don't screw it up!", I remarked.

By the first week of December our calendar was getting rather full with holiday events coming up. Andy and Alisha would be over to spend several weekends with us. Our other son, Ben, would come to spend some time with us too. In the meantime, we received a call from our middle son, David. He wanted us to come over and see the new wood laminate floor he laid in their living room. April had put up the Christmas tree and would like us to come for dinner. The date was set. He thought it would be fun to make some sugar cookies too. "Please bring cookie cutters!". "Okay!"

I called David a few days before hand to confirm the time. At the end of the conversation he said, "By the way, Momma, I was thinking about gingerbread cookies. Maybe we could make them like we used to." "Sure son."

I found my old recipe for gingerbread cookies and looked to see if I had all of the ingredients I was going to need to take to David and April's. Most of the recipe called for household ingredients. We were going to need just one special ingredient. Molasses. We would need a whole jar of molasses.

The son we hardly ever got to see, just happened to change his mind at the last minute and decided he wanted to bake gingerbread cookies with his Momma like he did when he was little, and we were going to need molasses.

I got it.

And I get it.

AN ANGEL AMONG US!

It was the fall of 2010. We had bought and settled into a nice little home in a suburb. We set off for a walk on one Sunday morning shortly before noon. There were a couple of ladies holding a yard sale. I said to Mark, "Honey, let's stop and look at their sale. People like it when you take an interest in their wares. It cheers them up!"

We walked up and said hello as we started looking around. After a few minutes of chit chat, we found a couple of things to come back for. One of the ladies commented on how cute we were together. That was all I needed to start preaching!

"That is because we are the head and not the tail! What God put together no man can put asunder! We are God's children and He loves His children!" I smiled.

They laughed and we ended the conversation saying we would be back in a few minutes. When we got back home my husband informed me he was going to take a shower. If I would, could I please go back and pick up the items without him. I said sure. I drove back with the money.

As I was paying the young lady named Lisa, I asked her what church she attended. She told me and then said she could not go regularly because of the pain she was in and everything she had wrong with her. She told me her story with all her diagnoses. This was a young woman sitting before me with a short time line.

Lisa's friend, who had been sitting with her when we first walked up earlier that morning, was now walking back over from her home. She said to Lisa while sitting down in her seat, "This is your angel. She is going to bring church to you. I knew she would come back and pray for you."

I knew then what I was really there for. "Lisa", I said, "Would you like me to pray for you right now?" She nodded her head yes putting her hands in her lap and closed her eyes. While her friend waited on the people at the yard sale, I put a hand on Lisa's back, my other hand on her lungs. I started praying. I asked for God's intercession by the holy and mighty name of Jesus for her. I prayed just a few minutes. Lisa looked up at me and smiled.

"I feel a little better already," she claimed. I gave her our phone number, and told her to call anytime. We would be looking for the good report. We hugged as sisters.

I came back home and told Mark what took so long. He smiled and was not surprised that I was about my Father's business.

You know, dear readers, this is your business too.

MINISTERING ANGELS

As I have stated before, we can all be angels in each others lives. We should all be about our Father's work. Sometimes, we are the ones who need to be ministered to. This was a time such as that.

Picking your life up and putting the pieces back together after great losses (job, family member, life experience), usually takes a little while. It had been three years since such a loss occurred in my life, and I had done everything from scrubbing floors and housekeeping to working at a health care clinic signing in patients. I went back to school to finish for a medical assistant through the winter of 2010, finishing up clinical rotations by the end of March.

Our friends, David and Dianna Gething, from England came to visit us over Easter. We had a lovely seven day visit and started plans for the next vacation together.

Two hours after we put them on a plane to go back home, we were at a closing for our first home in almost four years. It took a month to settle in.

All through the summer, I looked for a job. I put out over 50 calls, and applications, interviews, call backs, etc. Several were "shoe in's". But to no avail. Something happened every time. "We decided not to expand our business", "Medicare changed a ruling and we can't use you", "We decided not to hire as many people as we had originally anticipated", all the doors closed. Until the first week of July. It was starting to feel like God had another avenue for me to explore other than the 9 to 5 routine. I started praying, "All right Lord, You have closed every door I have tried to open. Show me what You want me to do."

On a Wednesday afternoon, my friend Karen called me from her busy office in the medical field. She is such a bright spot in our lives, I am always happy to take her call. She wanted to tell me about my "helper ministry". She wanted to set my head straight and for me to see what she sees. She is such an articulate, gifted, intelligent lady, when she speaks, I listen. (Just in case I'm missing something.) She said that I minister more in people's lives than anyone else she knows and that I should count that as a major gift. I thanked her for her insight.

That night, at bible study, my friend Clare told me that God has His hand on my ministry. Friends, I did not know I had a ministry.

The next night Mark and I were at the Ward's, another church member's home. They made clear to me what my ministry was. Holly said she saw God in me, that deep capacity to love unconditionally and real kindness towards others.

I prayed that weekend. I asked simply, "What do you want?" I received a one word reply. *OBEDIENCE.* That Monday I said yes to the Lord's ministry.

ORDER MY STEPS, LORD
Part One

It was less than a week after I said yes to the Lord's ministry. I was listening full time now. As the song says, *"No turning back."*

I was in our local grocery store when a little old couple came around the corner. I heard loudly in my head, ***"THIS IS IT!"*** I had instant knowledge. I knew the lady was battling cancer, and that she was a Catholic. She needed prayer right now!

I put my purse in my cart and walked over to her. I started out saying, "Excuse me, I know you don't know me, but do you have cancer?" The couple exchanged glances and she replied, "Yes, I do." I asked her if I could pray over her. She exclaimed, "Oh, yes! Please!" I started the prayer in Latin, then I asked for the power of the blood of Jesus to come down and replace her cancerous blood with Jesus blood.

They thanked me very much for obeying the Holy Spirit. We hugged and went on our own ways.

It looked like I got an "A" on my first assignment in obedience.

Our Pastor, Fred Schuppert calls this "pressing in". Pressure comes when we have to step out in God's knowledge, going against our own, but the rewards are heart felt and great!

ORDER MY STEPS, LORD
Part Two

By the end of the second week of July, and I had asked God every day to order my steps. He had, everyday.

Now, it was a Sunday evening, and no one on this day had come across my path to help or heal. Mark and I were at 6 pm church services. A lady was sitting across from me in the other aisle. I smiled at her. She smiled back. I felt in my spirit, a call out, *"Deep Sorrow."*

I went over and hugged her hello. I asked if she was okay. She said she was fine. I went back and sat down in my chair. Again, I heard louder, *"Deep Sorrow."*

I went back to where she was sitting, I got down on bended knees and looked up into her eyes. She looked at me and said, "You know, don't you?"

I said, "Yes."

She responded, "I asked God to send me someone to help me. He has sent me you."

A VISIT WITH CLARE

Clare and I set up a time ten days later to visit. I'm believing that God had sent me to her because her heart aches over a dispute. I invited her for an afternoon visit and a meal before going to bible study with my husband and I that evening.

She has a commanding presence physically and spiritually. In a pair of casual shoes, she stands almost six feet tall, with dark brown hair, and an effervescent smile. She is a very attractive lady, and easily liked.

She is blessed with many spiritual gifts as well. She listens and interprets accurately. I was anxious to hear stories unfold of all that she has seen and done over the years. Healing and prophesy are second nature to her. We were privileged to have her in our new home.

While talking and getting to know one another. I told her about our land and asked her if she would like to see it. She said yes. Wasting not a moment, we got in her car and headed in that direction. We were talking the whole way over.

When we turned onto the road that takes us to our subdivision, out of my mouth, never checked in with my head, I said, " **Now back here is where we live.**" This was out of my spirit, out of my mouth, then my ears and brain received it. This was a Holy Spirit revelation. I said, "Oh my, what did I just say?" Clare repeated it.

She started praying in tongues and English. She started prophesying in her spirit out loud, "House paid for with miracle money. Debt cancellation. In Jesus name. Angels perform this."

We got to our land a few minutes later. We stood where we want our home. She said, "Don't say anything. This is what I do best."

211

She saw in her spirit the original home we wanted to build. She started describing what she was seeing. She saw a big window in the back with a covered enclosed porch facing the hills and horse farms around us. This was without me telling her anything. This was her gift from God. She then said, "Don't worry. Pray without worry. Write down specifically what you want. Something is cooking from God for you. Don't give up hope. Oh, stop looking for a job."

I agreed to do so.

What ever this was, it was going to have to come to me.

THE HEALING OF BENJAMIN

Part One

A few days later Clare invited me out to lunch. The conversation was engaging, and the lunch was tasty. We came back to my home and spent the last few hours together between the living room and the kitchen where I was again preparing a meal. The last minutes of our meeting, this conversation came up.

She had once dated my ex-husband when she was a teenager. Then she gasped. It was as if she could see before her eyes all that had happened to me with him. The attack on me and his part in it. She stopped and asked me point blank, "Who carries this pain? Someone close to you knows. This is a deep dark depression over them. Ooohhhh, it's great. Who knows about this?" I started sobbing, "I think Ben knows. Clarence told him." She went into the spirit realm. "Deep anguish, heavy grief," she panted, feeling his pain. She started praying for Ben. She said, "This is why he can't receive Jesus." I moaned out loud!

Clare rebuked it all and cast it out of him in agreement with me. She felt it come off of him. She said we will see the fruit of this quickly.

That night at 11:15 pm, Ben came over unexpectedly to get some books he had ordered. Mark and I were already in bed. He bent down and kissed us and told us we were wonderful. He looked like he had weight lifted off his shoulders. He looked peaceful.

I smiled.

THE HEALING OF BENJAMIN

Part Two

The next evening at a hymn sing, Mark and I were talking with Pastor Kevin. We reminded him we have three sons. He started prophesying about all of them. "Call all things as if they already are. We call Ben a mighty man of God." He saw a ministry (heart) for people for him.

At 10:20 that evening I was standing by the phone at our home and Ben called. The first words he said to me were, "Momma, you were standing by the phone waiting for my call weren't you?" I stammered, "How did you know?" "I just knew," he replied. This was fruit of the spirit, word of knowledge coming to him. He started asking me questions about Jesus. And he already had all the right answers!

He said to me, "Didn't Jesus take on the sins of the world on the cross because he had to go to the cross blameless with no sin?" "Yes, son, that's right", I respond.

"Thanks Momma", he replied, " Well, we are getting back to studying our bibles now. I love you so much!"

I love you so much too, son.

THE HEALING OF BENJAMIN

Part Three

The only ones who knew we were praying for Ben were Clare and Pastor Kevin. So when I got a call the very next day from my friend, Deb Grimes about this subject, I knew God had pulled out all the stoppers to heal our son! God was calling in Catholic and Protestant prophets. It was Ben's time.

Deb started the conversation, "I have a word for Ben from Father Bernie. Tell him he can't fully receive the Holy Spirit with hate in his heart. That is what is standing in his way. When he lets it all go, he will receive the Holy Spirit in full." She felt this was to be a confirmation to us for Ben.

I started crying and told her all that I had already heard and that she was right. This was indeed a confirmation. I thanked her very much for being an obedient daughter of God.

AN ASSEMBLY OF ANGELS!

August of 2010 was an amazing time in our lives. This was just more proof to us that there is no such thing as coincidence!

Lots of times when you agree to become part of the Lord's Army, satan goes on the attack to cause distress and disbelief in your life. No different with ours.

By mid-August, I was full out doing good deeds , Mark and myself, everyday for people. It was almost as if they were coming out of the wood work!

Then the tide turned. We were the ones who need-ed help! Within a seven day period, two of my tires blew while the car was in the driveway, the computer crashed due to an electrical storm, and then I started having bad chest, stomach, arm and back pain. We had no money to fix any of these things.

Mark was worried his wife was having a heart attack. Mark's wife was worried she was having a heart attack! We knew satan was on the attack! We came together in agreeing prayer. We prayed and prayed.

Then, all of a sudden, a series of miracles started happening. As everything fell apart in one week, it all went back together in one week.

And the ending, was the best story of all . . .

AN ASSEMBLY OF ANGELS

MIRACLE # 1

When the computer blew", we thought we lost everything on it. A hunk of junk, after all, we had claimed it's final reward several times.

Mark called his brother, David at the beginning of the week to see if he could try to fix it once again. David said to bring it over later in the week, and he would see what he could do. It did not sound very promising.

By the end of the week, much to our surprise, David was able to not only fix it, but bring most of the information back up! The doctor of computer diagnosis had done it again and there was no charge for his services! It did not cost us a thing!

Yes we thanked God and David.

MIRACLE # 2

On Tuesday night of the same week, we told our pastor while at the singing engagement we were helping him at, that we were going to have to sell our topper off our truck to make ends meet this month due to all the things we've just had go wrong.

Well, it was settled right then and there between Pastor Schuppert and his wife, Jeanne, the church was buying the topper. Our truck does a lot of hauling for Believer's Fellowship, and it's only right that the church buy it and allow us to keep it on our truck. We sold the topper and got to keep it!

That was grocery money for the rest of the month!

AN ASSEMBLY OF ANGELS

MIRACLE # 3

Following that awful week, I was making a nice meal for my husband. I know, I am always cooking or ironing in these stories. I was still having unresolved chest and shoulder pain. It must be all the cooking and ironing I'm doing.

When my cousin Gail called "Deb!", she hollered into the phone, "I just bought the prettiest car I've ever had! I bought a $50,000.00 car for $15,000.00." Without missing a beat in the conversation, I replied, "Is it hot?" She laughed and gave me the short version. "No," she said, "I'm blessed." In the middle of my chest pain and no tires on my car, she wanted to come over and show me her good fortune. "Sure, come on over," I sigh, "I'm making a nice meal tonight, you can stay for dinner."

She showed up after work and took me for a drive around the block. Yes, it was a very nice car! She joined me in the house to have dinner with us. She talked to me in the kitchen while I was finishing up dinner. "What have you been doing lately? Where have you been going?", she asked me. I replied, " Well, not much of anywhere. The car is down." She asked, "What's wrong with your car?" I told her I had two blown tires and couldn't go anywhere. She asked me how much it would be to fix them. I told her some over $200.00. "Well, Deb," she started, "Why don't you go buy them? Don't you have $200.00?" She looked at me as if she didn't understand the problem. I couldn't make any words come out of my mouth. I just kept fixing dinner.

She asked me again, "Do you have any money?"

Again, my heart won't allow me to respond. She took $200.00 out of her pocket book and said to me, "Go get your tires. You'll see, it will come back to me seven fold."

Mark and I thanked her over and over again at the dinner table. We plan to pay them back by Mark helping Mike, Gail's husband on some projects he had going. It sounded like a deal for both of us.

AN ASSEMBLY OF ANGELS

MIRACLE #4

Before dinner was over, we got a call from my dear friend, Deb Grimes. She said, "Deb, can you do me a favor?" "Sure," I replied, "What do you need?" "I need you to go with me and my son to a Bats game. We have four tickets, and we hate to let them go to waste, " she states. "Alright," I said, "When is it?" "Tonight. We'll pick you up in half an hour. See you shortly!", she said brightly.

"Uh, Mark, honey," I started giggling, "we are being blessed with tickets to the Bats game!" He was excited since he has never been to see one. "Well wonderful! When is it?" he asked. "In a half hour, dear." I replied. Gail started laughing and said, "I guess we better finish up dinner quick! You people are busy!" We cleaned up the table and walked Gail to her new car. As she drove off in one direction, here came Deb and Brian from the other direction.

I was really not feeling up to going to a baseball game and in my heart I asked the Lord why He was having us go to a ball game that night. Already the answer was forming in my head. I knew there was more to the story about why we were going than met the eye. We got there just in time for the game to start!

All through the evening I was feeling worse. By the 6th inning I couldn't take it anymore. I asked Mark to help me to a first aid station. Maybe they would have some Tums they could give me.

We found the first aid station back a hallway. There were three very nice male EMT's and Paramedics. I went in and told them what I was feeling. They

220

worked for the very same ambulance company our son Andy worked for. The older gentleman knew him. He was one of Andy's supervisor's. I told him my background as a medical assistant and specialty in wellness. I asked them to give me the "once over". They did. My blood pressure was fine. My heart rate was fine. They didn't have any Tums. Sorry. They asked to hook me up to a 3-lead EKG. I agreed.

They started documenting procedure protocol. My heart rate went up as they hooked me up. The paramedic looked puzzled. I laughed and replied, "Sure my rate's up. Your hooking me up to a 3-lead. Natural response!" We laughed and watched the monitor for signs of electrical problems. It all came out clear. The heart was fine. They recommended a strong OTC medication for the stomach. Watch my diet. We went back to our seats and told Deb I was fine. It was just my stomach! We exclaimed how good God is! I just got free care that would have cost us several thousand dollars!

When Deb and Brian dropped us off at home later that evening, we went to our local pharmacy to see how much the medicine was. It was so expensive, we couldn't buy it.

Wait on God.

AN ASSEMBLY OF ANGELS

MIRACLE # 5

Two days later on a Friday, Mark and I went over to help our friends, Kaelin and Marie to cook for a bible study at our old home on Mathis Road. We ate lunch together, and it did not sit well with me. I ended up back in pain in my stomach and chest. I asked if my friends could pray for me. "Before everyone gets here for dinner tonight, we will stop and pray for your pain," brother Scully responded.

In the meantime, Mark went downstairs to get something out of the refrigerator. Marie went too. She came back upstairs saying she forgot something at the store. Could Mark please go get it for her. Absolutely. Mark made a trip to Wal-mart while I stayed and cut up vegetables for several dishes we were preparing. When Mark got back from the store he handed me the medicine we had said was too expensive.

He said, "Marie wanted to bless you with this." I told him I would take it later. Shortly after that brother Kaelin called us together for prayer. He prayed a simple prayer of faith over me with all of us in agreement.

In the same house that my back was instantaneously healed at, all the pain in my chest, stomach, neck and back left. It has never been back since. My second miracle in that blessed home.

The medicine is still unopened in our kitchen cabinet.

One more day remained in this beautiful week.

222

AN ASSEMBLY OF ANGELS
MIRACLE # 6

There I was on a Saturday morning with $50.00 for groceries and ten dollars for toilet paper. Oh boy! I now have a fixed tummy and computer, and I could now drive to the grocery on my new tires! What a week!

I stopped at the Family Dollar to pick up the toilet paper first. Except for a little detour. My feet didn't take me to the toilet paper aisle. My feet took me straight to the baby clothes aisle. I was thinking I've lost my mind. What was I doing in the baby aisle?!

Hey! They are having a sale! Three and four piece outfits, name brands, Disney and Blue the Dog, selling whole outfits for one and two dollars! Gail McCullum came immediately to mind! My cousin was having four new grand babies in the next five months!

I ran over to the counter and asked if I could use their phone! It was an emergency! Men won't get this but women will understand! I called her at her store just a half mile up the road. "Gail!", I hollered in the phone, "You have to get over to the Family Dollar right away! Hurry! They are selling name brand four piece outfits for baby's for one and two dollars!" "Deb! I have no car!" she groans, " Mike is gone on a job site, and I'm sitting her with my dad and no car!"

I went into action! "Get your purse ready. Let your dad watch the store, I'm coming to get you"! If I'd had a horn, I would have been blowing it all the way to her store! Watch how funny and good God is.

The lady who had no car tires, got blessed with tires so she could go to the store, see this tremendous sale that would bless the person who gave her the money for the tires, but, Gail had no car to get there, so, the lady she

223

bought the tires for came to pick her up and take her to the sale. And saved her a thousand dollars! Did you get all that?

We laughed and cried. She said to me in the store, "See? I told you God would bless me seven times over. You can't out give God! Thank you, Deb for being an obedient steward and listening to God. It was well worth the $200.00 that I spent for your tires!" I took her back to her store after shopping and dropped her and all her packages off.

I still needed to go to the grocery store.

God still had one more miracle to do there!

AN ASSEMBLY OF ANGELS

MIRACLE # 7
Order My Steps, Lord!

I walked into the grocery store thinking about how God had brought everything full circle. I could hardly wait to tell my husband, Mark, later in the afternoon.

I saw my friend, Karen, inside shopping. She invited us to her youngest son's birthday party that night. It will be nice to join them later at the church.

In the bread aisle of the Jay C store, I saw Pastor Kevin Mallory coming down the aisle. He was a local Methodist minister. We greeted each other with big smiles and hugs. We talked a little bit. His Momma was in town, and he was picking up some fried chicken for dinner that night. I gave him a praise report on how God furnished us free; our computer fixed, two new tires, grocery money, health care for my heart and stomach! All in one week!

I was thinking he would be happy for us. What he heard in his spirit and in his heart was lack for basic needs. The message I thought I was sending was not the one he was receiving.

He looked deep into my eyes. Then he started claiming scriptures over me and my husband and our sons. I asked him, "Is this from your heart or from the Lord?"

The Holy Spirit came over him and he started prophesying from God!

"Daughter, I call you daughter in whom I am well pleased!" At this point I was crying. He went on, "I have seen every good thing you have done in My name. I will reward you. Soon! In more than you have asked me for.

225

Your position is higher and you will have more than you need."

I was balling. Kevin was crying. I cried out, "He called me daughter! He called me daughter!" We went into praise, hands raised and glorifying God. Kevin invited us to his church social the next day and we had a lovely time. He invited us to his wedding in September. It was beautiful!

No one else came down the bread aisle while we were praying.

September brought the biggest surprise of all. That was when the idea of the book came together from four people in two different churches. Glory to God!

SUSAN'S CHRISTMAS SURPRISE

I am blessed with five wonderful sisters in-law on my husband's side of the family. This is a story about one of them.

Susan is an amazing lady. She is intelligent and beautiful and has a great job. Over the thirteen years I have known her, I haven't found anything she can't do well. She sews like a dream! She is a very gifted lady.

Susan is a devout Catholic. She prays and loves Jesus with all her heart. Most things go well for her. As a Catholic, she believes some people do have crosses to bear. Hers, over the last several years, has been her health. It has not been as well as she would like with several ongoing issues. But, like the trooper she is, she marches on through it as health and healing make their way back to her body.

Susan, like us, does not believe in coincidence. So, on Christmas morning, 2010, when she went out to warm up her car to go to breakfast at Mom's, she saw her Heavenly Father had been up to something. It had snowed the night before. Everything was glistening white. All the cars in the parking lot of the apartment complex sat still. No tracks were found around her car in the snow.

But on her car, on the hood of a completely cold car, was a smiley face.

A perfectly shaped, melted in place, happy face.

Of course, she smiled back.

Christmas Chaos
A Christmas Present
For Ben, Davey and Andy

It was the night before Christmas
in the Peyron house.
Not a boy child was stirring,
not even their pet mouse.

Their socks were all thrown,
and strewn all about.
We hoped that St. Nicholas
would not trip up or shout.

The children were wrestled and
tossed in their beds.
It was all the fudge and hot cocoa,
it danced in their heads.

As Momma and Dad at last
settled down to sleep,
the last words from Father were,
"I'll hear not a peep."

Yet, later in the yard,
there arose such a clatter,
with three teenage boys,
we knew something was the matter!

Away to the front door
 we flew like a flash,
the oldest had tore off a shutter
and made a big gash!

The full moon's light
 on the new fallen snow,
showed just what they had been up to,
and where they intended to go.

What to our amazed eyes
did appear,
they were sitting in a sleigh,
on top of eight tiny reindeer!

Even though the driver
 had been lively and quick,
I knew in a moment,
they had beat up St. Nick!

Faster than eagles,
 we joined in this game,
We hollered and shouted
 and called them by name!

Now Benjamin! David!
 Even Andy, you too?!
What are we going to do
 with this unruly crew?

They hung their heads low,
on this there's no doubt,
as they blamed each other quickly,
and all started to pout.

But our order's were clear,
up to their bedroom's we'd send,
and have to figure out,
how all this, we would amend.

"Apologize to Santa,
help pick up his toys!
Show him you can still be
our good little boys!"

"Come on, St. Nick,
 you're in no shape for the roof."
The reindeer agreed, pawing the ground
with each little hoof.

We brought him inside
and setting him down,
"No more chimneys tonight my friend,
we're your last stop in this little town!"

He was distressed all the way
from his head to his foot.
His fur was torn and tattered,
with dirt and with soot.

The bag was all tore
that he had flung on his back,
Nick looked like a peddler,
who'd been in a high jack!

His eyes could still focus,
as he tried to be merry,
but his cheek was slightly swollen,
so we offered him a sherry.

His mouth too had been hit,
It had drawn up quite nice,
so I ran to the kitchen
to get a bag of crushed ice.

He asked for his pipe,
even though they loosened one of his teeth.
We found it outside,
wedged under our front door's wreath.

Nick soon relaxed,
his nerves did take hold.
Finally my husband asked,
being overly bold,

"Santa, this was a mistake.
I'm sure our boys meant no real harm.
Will you still leave something for our loved ones,
here on this small farm?"

By this time, Nick was back
to feeling a jolly old elf.
We all laughed together,
in spite of ourself!

A wink of his eye,
and he could still turn his head,
soon led us to know
we had nothing to dread!

He smiled and got up,
He went straight to his work.
He filled all our stockings,
and turned without a jerk.

Before he could leave,
we held our hands out to pray,
for the rest of his commute,
that safe he would stay.

This touched his heart so,
prayer was not much found in this land,
"How do you know of this?" he asked,
as he held out his hand.

"Our Jesus in the Bible,
tells us all true,
that He lived and died for us,
for me and for you.

This is why forgiveness is for us,
and our boys.
Jesus has already come for us,
with a trump and a noise!

Peace is for here and for now,
that is the Word.
Our Christian Bible teaches it,
this much we have heard."

Nicholas smiled as he left our home
and he drove out of sight.
He called "Merry Christ's Mass to all!
And to all a blessed night!"

Love,
Momma

December   2010

MARK'S TESTIMONY

As a child growing up in the country with little direction that I listened to, and by that I mean my dad was gone building his business and my mom was busy with my brother and four sisters, I was allowed to run and be out of the house most days that were fit. Even though Dad was out and mom was busy, I knew they loved me. I felt it. They did all the right things, like hugs and kisses, three meals a day, regular bedtimes, don't waste things or food, chores, being told when I did a good job and thanked for it. Spanked when all else failed. We all received extra love and care when we were ill. We went to church and Sunday School.

Growing up in the Roman Catholic Church , I had no understanding of Latin. I missed out on a lot of God's word in my early years. I did learn that God loved me and that love was so great that he sent His son Jesus, who is forgiveness of sin and the promise of everlasting life, to be crucified and raised on the third day. Even though I knew that is what happened and I believed it, I did not know or accept what that meant for me.

As I grew up I did many foolish, stupid and dangerous things. That mind set followed me into young adulthood. Many still choose the path of lack of morals, alcohol and drugs. Where's the next party mentality. God calls this the path of destruction.

I was married and divorced when I was 24 years old to a "party girlfriend". Then I married again at 30 thinking I would be married the rest of my life. We did not go to church, and I hardly gave God a nod. I was divorced again by the age of 34. I did not want to be divorced this time, and I took it very hard. I sometimes wonder what effect we have on God when we reject His love for us.

233

During the first year after the divorce, I lost 65 pounds. I was so broken and depressed, I could not see anyway out. Only darkness. That was when I decided to take my own life. That day at the kitchen table with my head in my hands sobbing, I cried out to God. As I was getting up to fulfill my decision, at that moment the phone rang. It was my sister Susan. I don't remember anything we talked about or how long we talked, but God used her to break the spirit of suicide on me. I knew I cried out to God, He heard me and He did something. He must love me!

Now I must stop here, dear reader. If you are thinking suicide is your way out of the little box that depression has painted you in, **IT'S NOT!** In Hosea 4: 6 The word of God says My people are destroyed for lack of knowledge. I would have taken my own life not knowing I could trust God. When I cried out to Him, He broke the spirit of death I had invited into myself. God loves you jut as much as he loves me. Call out to God, trust in Him. He will answer you. Listen for Him. He will reach out to save you. He tells us the same thing He told Peter. "Come."

Peter got out of the boat and walked on the water. Then he took his mind off Jesus and fear came. Matt 14:31 "And **immediately** Jesus caught him." Don't deny Him when He answers. God has an unlimited number of ways to reach you. How many times has God already reached out to you?

I slowly started to feel better. In the fall of 1994 I had a dream that changed me. It was one of those dreams that was so vivid I remembered every small detail of it to this day. I know this is from the Lord. I dreamed I was driving down a country road following a utility work truck. A neatly bound bundle of rope flew out of the back of the truck off to the right side of the road. I then drove

234

off the road onto a leaf covered path into the woods. I drove up to a very large tree. I got out of the car and climbed to the top of the tree, standing on the leaves. I looked down at my feet, and I see a hole in the leaves of the tree. I reached in and pulled out a five inch tall statue of the Virgin Mary. It was very dusty and dirty. I cleaned it up and put it in my jacket pocket. I reached into the same hole again and pulled out a statue of Saint Joseph. It too was dusty and dirty so I cleaned it and put it in my jacket pocket too. Then another car drove up to the tree, and three men got out and climbed up the tree just that fast to about ten feet below me.

One was closer than the other two. He looked at me and said, "Get out of my tree." as he threw down an extension ladder that was between us. He told me a second time to get out of his tree. I said, "Wow! I've never seen anyone climb a tree that fast!" I looked at him. He wore a black hooded jacket. He had coal black eyes full of anger and hate in his face. A third time he told me to get out of his tree. When I began to step over the edge of the tree I woke up.

Two weeks later, I had another dream. I had just come home from work, and there was a package in the mail for me. I took it inside and opened it to find the same two statues of the Mother of Jesus and the earthly Father of Jesus.

I knew God was calling me in a way I could understand. Before too long I was going back to church occasionally. At this time I was 37 years old. I knew that God loved me. I also knew that I wanted to know all that I could about God and what He wanted for me. I decided to seek God. Everyday I did something to feed my hunger to know the Lord. I would read my bible, or listen to Christian talk radio, and I would pray and ask God to help me. We all need God's help.

Daily, moment to moment there is a fight going on inside each of us between our flesh and our spirit. Romans 8 is a wonderful discussion of this fight and what our life in Christ can do for us. The word of God says to renew our minds. We do that by studying and reading our bibles, as well as with prayer and paying attention to how God is showing Himself to us.

In April of 1995 I was baptized in the Holy Spirit. I woke up that morning with the most wonderful feeling of being weightless. It was as if every burden I had was lifted off my shoulders. Just like I was walking on air.

For the next hour I sang in tongues. I knew nothing about tongues at that time. I believe that experience was a gift from God as a way of saying keep coming. I'm here. Shortly after I started to make changes in my life. I stopped dating. I starting listening to more Christian talk radio and going to church much more.

In November of 1997 at a Catholic Singles function at one of my neighbor's home, I met my wife to be, Debbie. We talked a lot and seemed to have much in common. I gave her my phone number, and two weeks later she called me.

Our first date she took me to a Baptist Church in Louisville, Kentucky. It was an event called "Walk through Bethlehem". It was a reenactment of when our Savior was born.

Our second date was to her Charismatic Catholic prayer group in Lanesville Indiana. That is where she tried to fix me up with her long time friend, Mary. I put a stop to that notion. Her prayer group was my first experience with charismatic Catholics. They are a group of spirit filled people that love Jesus. They meet every Thursday to Praise God. There was another man there named Mark who sang beautiful love songs to God in tongues.

I immediately liked them. And what they were doing. I could feel the love of Jesus in them. They are each beautiful brothers and sisters in Christ.

Now back to Debbie wanting to fix me up with her friend. As you have read in her stories of her life, she did not have a lot of trust in men or what they had to say. And, I don't blame her. I knew that she was special, and I wanted to know her better. I am a patient man. I was also a bit afraid. I was self employed and did not know if I could afford to care for a sick wife with three little boys. I prayed and God gave me peace about the relationship. I still tried to fight it, and we broke up for one month.

There was no peace in that.

In August of 1999 we got married and moved to Corydon, Indiana. Before Deb and I married, we had a bowling date with her three boys. When the oldest boy, Ben, hit a strike, we did a "high five" and it clicked a memory of a dream I had doing that very same thing over two years before.

Now I believe that because we moved to Corydon and met our doctor and dear friend, Michael Bonacum, we saved Debbie's life. I thank God for all the wonderful doctors who take time with their patients. Also for the truth in the word of God that builds faith and supernatural power that can heal any sickness, disease or disorder that comes against believer's.

In June of 2001 the Billy Graham Crusade came to Papa John's Stadium in Louisville, Kentucky. Deb and I went to three of the meetings. On one with our sons Andy and Ben, we all went forward for the alter call. I had for some time wanted to make a public confession that Jesus Christ is my Lord and Savior. Like many that night, I went forward and received the gift of salvation in Christ Jesus.

237

I was met by a nice man named Dave. He led me in the sinners prayer. I accepted the gift of salvation. And what a gift it is! Dave gave me a card I still carry. It reads: *My decision for Christ. Knowing that I need the Lord Jesus Christ as my savior, I now trust in Him to pardon and deliver me from the guilt and power of sin. As he gives me strength I shall witness for Him, serve Him in the fellowship of His church, and seek to do His will in all areas of my daily life.*

> *God said it...........In His word*
> *I believe it...........In my heart*
> *That settles it......Forever!*

That little card said it all. My decision for Christ. For several years, before this day, I had a longing in my heart to make a public claim that I accept Jesus as my savior. My sins are now forgiven forever. Romans chapter 8 is one of my favorite chapters in the Bible. Verse one states, "There is now no condemnation to them which are in Christ Jesus, who walk not after the flesh, but after the spirit." Verse two states, "For the law of the spirit of life in Christ Jesus hath made me free from the law of sin and death."

Now, saints, listen, I have failed so many times in this battle of the flesh and spirit. I have been tripped up for years at some points in my life. And I know many of you have also. We are all so very saturated with the words of the world which are against the word of God, that we become fertile ground for the devil to plant and reap a harvest of misery in our lives. I do believe you can be a born again believer and still be miserable if you don't get the word of God into your hearts! Get the word of God in your heart and mind, and you will get faster to recognize when you are about to get tripped up and fall for a lie.

I mentioned earlier how God said that his people

are destroyed for lack of knowledge. This lack can manifest in many different ways. None are good. People get sick and don't call out to God to heal them. Our churches don't teach that such things are possible anymore. We don't trust God the way He wants us to. More believers trust the world or the government or the doctor or the lawyer over the word of God.

God has asked us in His word to diligently seek Him. We need the weapons God supplies us to win in the battle with the flesh. Jesus said His words are spirit and life. In Hebrews 4:12 "For the word of God is quick, and powerful, and sharper than any two edged sword, piercing even to the dividing asunder of soul and spirit, and of the joints and marrow and is a discerner of the thoughts and intents of the heart". God says His word is a treasure and for us to hide it in our hearts. I most certainly believe that if we truly understood the word of God and received the indwelling of the Holy Spirit then we could do all things in Christ Jesus who strengthens us.

Dear Friend, I don't claim to know everything. I really only know a small portion of the massive multidimensional truth that God and His word are. The truth is that it was not that many years ago I had none of God's word in my heart. Everyday could be a day of evil and be tricked without the word of God in us.

Start today. Decide to choose God and choose life! Speak the words of life to yourself, and your family. Trust God and ask Him to help you. Then pay attention to what is going on around you. God has an unlimited number of ways to reach you. When I paid attention after prayer and contemplating God, I would see Him work even in the simplest things, He loves us that much!

Several years ago the man I work for asked me to go and cut the screen door at his mother-in-laws because

239

she had locked herself out of her home. As I drove up to her home I saw several adults and children there. I also noticed that the door was a glass wrought iron security door. I asked God, "Lord, how are we going to get in that door?" As I walked to the door, I was told how they had all tried several times to get in. So I pressed the handle button, and the door opened. Needless to say, they were all surprised and asked me how I did that. I told them I didn't do it. If that door was locked, it was God who unlocked it. To God be the glory!

Now I know this is a simple thing. But this is God. He wants to be part of our lives. He wants to help us with every problem from the small to the impossible. Pay attention to His reply!

Another time I worked a second job for several years for my youngest sister and her husband, Bette and Tim McCoy. They own and operate McCoy's Nursery and Landscape Company in Charlestown, Indiana. I would dig shrubs for them. This was on a beautiful September day, not a cloud in the sky all day, just a big rich royal blue sky. As I would dig I would pray for our children, for my friend Eva who was to have carpal tunnel surgery, and for my Uncle Bob who was about to be called home by Jesus. I prayed for sometime out loud and also quietly in my spirit. I asked God if He was hearing me. In my Spirit I asked Him to show me something. I waited a moment or two and went back to work and prayer. After about twenty minutes I felt I needed to turn around and look up. There was a cloud cross in a slight angle toward me. A perfectly formed cross in the sky!

Well I got a big smile on my face and started thanking God and praising Him for it. Almost immediately the enemy of all believers entered my thoughts and tried to say some natural explanation for the cross. This time I was quick to call him the liar that he is, and cast him out of my thoughts and went back to praising God! I paid attention to what was going on. You must pay attention too.

I know my wife has told you about her broken back. I think I felt as helpless as she did. It was one of the most terrible times in our married life. She suffered so much, and there was so little I could do to help. It seemed like what ever man did to help it only made her worse. We soon would spend all the money we had, and more bills still came in.

Throughout this ordeal with Deb's back, we would pray and pray. Fast and pray. It seemed like it was all for nothing. Have you ever wondered why God does what He does and when He does it? Through my prayers, I have come to a conclusion. Our lives are like a movie, and we can only see the part we are in. But God can see our entire life and every aspect of it. And all the people that are part of our lives and all the people in their lives, etc. I think when we are born again believers with the word of God in our hearts, God can direct us in "our movie." When God instantaneously healed Deb's back through our dear friend Lee, I felt that burden of fear and helplessness come off me. My heart was filled with joy for my wife. God is so very good to us.

Now Deb and I have been married over eleven years at this time. Throughout this time we have had great pain and great joy, spiritual highs and lows. Prayers that have gone seemingly unanswered to instantaneous permanent healing. It has been a wonderful journey as we have sought God in all that we do.

God tells us to diligently seek him. Start today for yourself. Get a bible, and a concordance and read. Pray and trust God to help you find your way to Him. He can work with you with that attitude. Listen saints, God does not want any of us to be lost. Seek Him, walk in faith, and if you fail, get back up, repent, turn to God again. Make up your mind to follow Jesus. We have our savior in Christ Jesus. He and He alone delivers us from destruction. Or danger or any trap that the devil sets. Jesus is our redeemer. He ransomed us. He made it possible for us as believers in faith to receive the Holy Spirit. To understand and use the word of God in our everyday lives. To get the victory over the devil and the words of the world.

Dear friend, with all my heart, I encourage you to pray for understanding as you read your bible. Talk to and trust in God, and please pay attention for God's reply!

In Christ's love,

Mark Allen Peyron

EPILOGUE

Jer: 29:11 *"For I know the plans I have for you, declares the Lord, plans to prosper you and not to harm you, plans to give you a hope and a future."*

Psalm 115:14 *"The Lord shall increase me more and more, me and my children."*

Now, what would I like you to understand from reading this book and for going on this journey with me? I'm going to ask you to think. Did you see any of yourself or your circumstances in here? Can you now see God's work in your life a little easier? How He is with you everyday too? I am asking for insight on your part here, within your heart and mind and spirit. I am asking you to look for the miracles that occur in your lives as well. Assuredly, if they are out there for me, many times on an everyday basis, they are out there for you too. God is no respecter of persons. What He does for one He will do for all who ask in His Son's name.

What wisdom can I give here that will help sustain you on your journey?

First, don't conjure up dead enemies. Every time you think of your past negative experiences, you give them power over your head and heart. Where do you think depression comes from? You want to beat depression? Start remembering the miracles God has performed just for you! Write them down. Understand that miracles didn't stop yesterday. They go on and on just like God. He is eternal. His energy is eternal. His love for you is eternal too.

243

Then call God's promises from the bible into your life. Make every problem's knee bow before God's goodness. God's promises in the bible are not only for you in Heaven, but for you right here and right now. What do I mean by now? **I mean now!** Go ahead! Plead the blood of Jesus over you and your family. It is His blood that sets you free. Free from sin, free from sickness, free from lack and even free from death! So, go ahead and ask for God's mercy and grace over you and all that you do.

I truly believe this is the age of miracles once again. That a miracle ministry is being given all over the earth to all who will accept it right now. This is why so many people seem to be at the right place at the right time. Take me for example. And my family.

And you too.

I have to believe the best is yet to be for those who fear and revere God. Call God's Holy Scriptures into your life. Know the word of God. Read it, and get it into your heart. Then use it as He shows you.

Agree with God that healing is coming back with power and glory!

Agree with God that your financial blessings are being restored!

Release the power of God that is in your spirit!

Writing this book was not a labor of love. This was an act of obedience, and my heart ached most days because of it. Sorrow may persist in the night but joy comes in the morning! And it did!

Remember when I told you Andy could smell "good" coming to people? He said he had a good feeling about everything for Mark and I. That God was cancelling out worry for us. I am sure this was done when Jesus was on the cross.

That means it is done for all of us.

Pastor Ivie heard for us, "Hang on tight! Your miracle is coming!" These were the same words that were given to me when I was waiting for my back to be restored.

I await the rest of my restoration. For me. For my family. For all of you. I truly believe good is out there for all of us. It is just waiting to be received. Let God restore you too.

Go to Him.

In the meantime, let's keep each other in our prayers.

Shalom! (Health, prosper and peace)

We hope you have enjoyed our journey together.
We look forward to you joining us again!

God has already inspired Deborah to write
more on these topics. Be sure to watch for
these books coming in the future:

Christmas Chaos
An illustrated children's Christmas story
told with humor, verse,
and Christ, of course.

Miraculous Interventions
Amazing stories from five different ministers who
walk in the miraculous. These will be their
experiences with the Lord and the Divine
interventions they have witnessed.

More Walking in the Supernatural
"The rest of the story"

Christmas Stories
Real life stories as well as fiction wrapped around
the Christmas theme.

Raising the Dead
Physically and Spiritually
True stories relating experiences in the paranormal
as God sees it.

We welcome you to share your comments and experiences with us like minded believers. These in this book have been written in order to encourage the brethren and inspire the secular world.

To contact us, send your email to:

debinyeshi@yahoo.com

or to the publisher at:

HomeCraftedArtistry@yahoo.com

or by U.S. Mail to:

Home Crafted Artistry & Printing
1252 Beechwood Avenue
New Albany, IN 47150

Made in the USA
Charleston, SC
24 June 2011